FULL EMPLOYMENT

# Full Employment

*edited by*

Michael Barratt Brown, Ken Coates,
Ken Fleet and John Hughes

Spokesman

First published in 1978



CLOTH ISBN 0 85124 217 0
PAPER ISBN 0 85124 218 0



Published by Spokesman
Bertrand Russell House, Gamble Street, Nottingham
Printed by the Russell Press Ltd., Nottingham

# Contents

# List of Tables

# PART ONE

## Introducing Mass Unemployment

# 1 Introduction

# The Abandonment of Full Employment

**Ken Coates**

Editor of *The Spokesman*, Ken Coates is Senior Tutor in Sociology at Nottingham University.

Those who remember the political issues of the early 'sixties will doubtless recollect the famous trade union agitation on unemployment, which culminated in a remarkable lobby of Parliament, during which hitherto unheard-of rumbustiousness took place in the precincts of the Palace of Westminster. At the time, the dole-queues numbered some 700,000, calculated on a more inclusive basis than that which is applied in the middle and later 'seventies.

Today, "official" unemployment runs at something over double what it was then. Of course, we have to allow for the use of a rubber measure. The inadequacy of the official count has frequently been discussed, and indeed it became a strong debating point during the lifetime of the Heath administration, when the Labour Party campaigned strenuously because there was reason to believe that concealed unemployment taken together with the Department of Employment figures had already passed the million mark. Indeed, the 1971 Census does reveal more than 300,000 unemployed persons over and above the officially acknowledged registered numbers.

The onset of slump, and the continuing and fundamental weakness of the British economy within the context of that slump, have already combined to take the statistics to a new high level. Facing this fact, and the linked apostasy of the Labour Government, which had, by the beginning of 1977, already reneged upon some of its major commitments for change, a group of economists and political activists met at Ruskin College in the Spring, and launched an appeal which was published in the socialist press during the following May.

The text of this appeal read as follows:

"Most of the major social and democratic advances which have been made in Britain since 1945 have been directly founded upon the fact that relatively full employment has prevailed for almost three decades. Upon this basis has been built a considerable development of social and community services, a notable advance of trade union organisation and influence, and a marked growth of self-confident democratic aspirations among large sections of the people.

For many years, also, there has been a fairly large area of ostensible political consensus, in which all major parties have insisted that they were firmly and permanently committed to the maintenance of a fully employed economy.

Today, all this has changed. When the present Government came to office, unemployment stood at approximately 600,000. Now it is nearly 1,400,000. But this fact, bad in itself, is not as serious as the more sinister underlying fact that the very idea of full employment has been officially abandoned as a practical option for the entire forseeable future.

Levels of unemployment between 1 million and 1,500,000 are now assumed to be inevitable by all the forecasts of economic performance, while more pessimistic predictions exist which anticipate levels reaching two million.

The Government has clearly based its current policy on the notion that this is now "acceptable", and has taken a whole series of measures which, unless they are reversed, will ensure that it becomes unavoidable. In its agreement with the International Monetary Fund, and in subsequent related policy decisions, the Government has directly withdrawn every major positive undertaking given to the trade unions during the negotiations which established the existing social contract, so that all the burdens accepted by wage-earners at that time will now be augmented by further heavy imposts as a direct result.

During the negotiations on the second stage of the contract, the Government had committed itself to a growth rate of 4 per cent. In the event, growth was restricted to 1 per cent. Informed estimates consider this shortfall to be the equivalent of 400,000 jobs.

Partly because the defensive strength of the unions makes dismissals and redundancies difficult to enforce, an extremely high proportion of the new unemployed are young people who have not been able to secure either jobs or union membership. To this circumstance may be traced a whole series of regressive pressures on the educational system, which unwind behind the unjustifiable reproach that, in some way, schools are responsible for the shrinkage of the job-market.

At the same time, although the unions have registered disquiet at the failure of the Government to honour its side of the social contract, the TUC as a whole has, so far, failed to present a clear balance-sheet to its affiliates, and has not given the lead which is needed to help unions face up to the problems which result.

Beyond doubt, the unions did not believe in 1976, that they were accepting a contract based upon rising unemployment, and they *cannot* ratify such a contract now.

Cuts in public expenditure – particularly severe in 1977 and 1978 – aggravate all these problems at the very moment when a controlled expansion and shift of public spending is necessary to ameliorate them.

At the level of the social policy, all kinds of harmful reactions are thus encouraged. Racism and ultra-Right-wing demagogy are stimulated. The centre of gravity of conventional politics is displaced away from liberal, socialist or democratic standards towards increasingly oppressive and arbitrary presumptions.

As the trade unions find themselves caught in the effect of a drastic shift of public policy, they will discover that many of their traditional powers are eroded. A weakening of trade unionism, were it allowed to pass unchallenged, would mean a weakening of all other forms of community action and self-defence, and an undermining of the democratic vitality of a far wider population than that immediately affected by savage cuts in public spending and increases in enforced idleness.

At the international level, the crisis has generated high unemployment levels in many other countries, including some which have previously been more or less committed to welfare policies. The institutions of the European Community have not been mobilised to make any concerted attack on the social problems which arise from unemployment, still less to concert serious attempts to enlarge the number of job opportunities.

While European trade unions have agreed in principle on important and relevant measures, such as the need for the 35-hour week, much remains to be done to advance such objectives in an urgent and practical way.

Regardless of the attitudes of the Brussels Commission, unions need to consider, at national and international levels, how far collective bargaining can be employed to generate new jobs. Among obvious solutions are the reduction of hours without loss of pay, the establishment of drastic reductions in the hours of workers on anti-social shifts, earlier retirement on generous terms in heavy industries, accelerated recruitment and improved training of new workers in order to maintain capacity in the face of such reforms, and bargaining for more apprenticeships, training and works experience, under union conditions and supportive union supervision, for the young.

Distressed by the social consequences of unemployment, and convinced that full employment remains a key political priority, the supporters of this appeal call upon democratic organisations, local political associations, trade unions and pressure groups to join in a widespread and careful discussion of the problems involved in the struggle for full employment, with the intention of agreeing upon an adequate programme of action to eliminate unemployment. Such action should include not only feasible policies for implementation at the level of Government, but also appropriate responses by trade unionists, local authorities and other associations. It should include remedies which can be pressed upon the authorities at both national and international levels.

To help to focus this discussion, we shall convene a national seminar during the month of July, which will commission a series of specialised reports from authorities, interest-groups, and qualified researchers, and establish a number of working parties to develop practical proposals within particular fields."[1]

As a result of this initiative, the seminar to which the appeal refers was held at Leicester University, and the present volume was edited from the papers submitted to that meeting.

---

1. *Signatories to Full Employment Appeal included:*

Norman Atkinson, MP, Sydney Bidwell MP, Norman Buchanan MP, Robin F. Cook MP, Bryan Davies MP, Geoff Edge MP, Martin Flannery MP, Brian Gould MP, Eric S. Heffer MP, Neil Kinnock MP, Joan Lestor MP, Max Madden MP, Jim Marshall MP, Joan Maynard MP, Ian Mikardo MP, Brian Sedgemore MP, Renee Short MP, Ron Thomas MP, Stan Thorne MP, Audrey Wise MP.

Colin M. Barnett (NUPE), Bernard Dix (NUPE), Jack Dunn (secretary Kent Area NUM), Moss Evans (general secretary elect, TGWU), Alan Fisher (general secretary, NUPE), Ken Gill, (general secretary, AUEW-TASS), Gerry Gillman (general secretary, SCPS), Walt Greendale (TGWU), David Hall (SCPS), Danny Harris (TGWU), P.E. Heathfield (secretary, Derbyshire area, NUM), Bill Jones (TGWU), Peter Jones (AUEW), Max Morris (NUT), Brian Nicholson (TGWU), Reg Race (NUPE), Ernie Roberts (AUEW), Alan Sapper (general secretary, ACTT), Bob Wright (assistant general secretary, AUEW), George Wright (regional secretary, Wales TGWU: general secretary, Wales TUC). (All in a personal capacity).

Michael Barratt Brown (Sheffield University), Stephen Bodington, Ken Coates (Nottingham University), Frank Field (Low Pay Unit), Ken Fleet (Institute for Workers' Control), Denis Gregory (Trade Union Research Unit, Ruskin College), Peter Hain (Young Liberals), Professor Royden Harrison (University of Warwick), Simon Hebditch (Young Liberals), Michael Hill (University of Bristol), Geoff

Hodgson (Manchester Polytechnic), Stuart Holland (Sussex University), John Hughes (Ruskin College), Dennis Marsden (University of Essex), John O'Malley (Canning Town Community Development Project), Eric Preston (ILP), Raphael Samuel (Ruskin College), Bill Silburn (University of Nottingham), Adrian Sinfield (University of Essex), E.P. Thompson, Dorothy Thompson, A.J. Topham (University of Hull), Professor Peter Townsend (University of Essex), Alan Walker (National Children's Bureau), Frank Wilkinson (University of Cambridge), Raymond Williams, Barry Winter (ILP).

The Institute for Workers' Control agreed to act as a postbox, and undertook the organisation of the Leicester seminar.

# 2 The Problem

## An Overview*

**Peter Townsend**

Professor Townsend is pro-Vice Chancellor of the University of Essex.

Until the late 1960s full employment seemed to be one of the first principles of Socialist philosophy, which seemed to distinguish the Labour movement from Tories in a fundamental way – even though full or high, employment had prevailed under successive Governments. It was a comfortable assumption, from which socialists were first rudely parted in 1967. In that year the average number of unemployed rose to over half a million without Labour Ministers being visibly alarmed or mortified. On the contrary, people were nursed into accepting a temporary higher level of unemployment as a necessary condition of economic recovery – especially in the speeches of Harold Wilson. That was territory surrendered without even a fight. The failure to defend full employment therefore has a history spanning ten years. A comprehension of that history is necessary to the development of a counter strategy.

While large scale unemployment has deeper roots, it also has a more complex structure, than is supposed in much political discussion. That structure is, of course, tied to the structure of employment and has to be unravelled and explained if any really effective employment policy is to be developed. A so-called full employment policy which created millions more lowly paid and insecure workers in an even more unequal occupational hierarchy, or conveniently labelled millions more unemployed and occupationally deprived people as dependent housewives, handi-

*A shorter version of this paper was published in the *New Statesman*, October 7th 1977, with the title, "The Neglect of Mass Unemployment"

capped or disabled and retired would not be worth the paper it was written on. Unemployment is only one aspect of insecurity and inequality in capitalist society and can only be understood in that context.

Why is the structure of unemployment so complex? Part of the answer is familiar or easily accepted, and is to do with age, duration of unemployment, employment history, level of skill and occupation class. Official unemployment is a phenomenon which disproportionately affects the young and late middle-aged. Of 1,622,000 unemployed in Britain in July 1977, 313,000 were under 18 and 708,000 under 25. Of these 708,000 as many as 134,000 had been unemployed continuously for more than six months. Yet the young are on the whole better educated, better qualified and longer educated than the middle-aged, and if we were to claim that unemployment was the result of deficient skills we would have to impugn the present systems of education and industrial training and not just the lack of retraining centres for people in middle life. And it is of course impossible to say that the unemployed could get jobs if they wanted to, since notified vacancies are currently little more than 10 per cent of total numbers unemployed. It is also important to note that the unemployment rate among the registered disabled is currently 14 per cent; that there are nearly as many people unemployed who are considered by the Department of Employment to be registrable as disabled as there are unemployed who are so registered, but that both registered and registered unemployed disabled account for only 9 per cent of the total unemployed.

In analysing unemployment the relationship with class is of considerable significance. The chances of being unemployed for those in the lower ranks of the occupational hierarchy and the unemployment rate among unskilled workers is very high. Studies of the unemployed in the last few years by Hill, Daniel and Marsden, and most recently in his evidence to the Royal Commission on the Distribution of Income and Wealth, by Geoff Norris, have demonstrated the vulnerability of those in occupations at the foot of the hierarchy not only to being unemployed at any particular time, but to having recurrent spells of unemployment, and part-time, seasonal and low paid employment. In July there were 431,000 general labourers on the registers of the unemployed, compared with 8,000 notified vacancies – or 53 unemployed men for every relevant job vacant. In this situation it is absurd for employers to refuse to consider for jobs men and women who have been out of work more than a few weeks.

But the disproportionately high rate of *current* unemployment among manual, and particularly unskilled, workers has to be related to the structure of insecurity as affecting manual workers. Jobs are more insecure, notice shorter, fringe benefits comparatively smaller or rarer, hours of work more often unsocial, conditions of work worse and risks of accident and death greater. The comfort and virtual unsackability of many non-manual staff and key skilled manual grades in a capitalist system is paid for both by a large number of marginal jobs and the dispensability of young people who have come into a system governed in part by the principle of seniority. Some jobs on the margins of those controlled by firms are added or terminated from time to time, depending on trends in economic fortunes. Correspondingly, people in work, especially in the lower manual grades, may experience occasional or successive spells off work or, at worst, long term unemployment. There are not two broad states of employment and unemployment, but a hierarchy of states from whole time secure employment through discontinuous employment to continuous unemployment. It is a continuum.

Socialists must also beware of restricted definitions of unemployment. Sir Keith Joseph and others have attempted to minimise its scale by trying to exclude from the total numbers categories of handicapped or sick people and those between jobs. The real problem is, however, not one of overestimation but underestimation. In addition to the registered unemployed there are those of working age who are looking for work but not registered at an exchange. The Census of 1971 found 400,000 more unemployed than were registered with the Department of Employment. In 1972 a Government inter-departmental working party conceded that there were at least an additional quarter of a million. We can regard that a quarter of a million as a minimum addition to the present numbers officially registered. There are other people of working age who would enter employment if there were more work available, or if conditions were right and society were to encourage it. The numbers of older men remaining at work has fallen dramatically in the last 20 years. There are large numbers of active people of pensionable age who would like, or be prepared to undertake, productive employment of some kind. Although the pension age is lower, for example, in the Soviet Union, deliberate encouragement of pensioners to work has been given, with the result that between 1964 and 1975 the number, both men and women working, has increased from 10 per cent to 24 per cent. Retirement for some is a euphemism for unemployment and current proposals to pension off more people in late middle-age are short-sighted expedients which ignore long-term problems of both a social and economic nature. Any acknowledgement of the overlap between our concepts of unemployment and retirement allows us to see more clearly that the definition of the *scope* of, and access to, employment is more a matter of social decision, after public consultation and debate, than a matter to be left to market forces. Our realisation of the *social* determinants of policy arises in part from the artificial divorce between the employed and retired populations at an arbitrary pension age, but also in the distribution of overtime work in a small labour force instead of developing incentives to retain a larger labour force. The redistribution, equalisation and reorganisation of work is as big a question for Socialists as the redistribution, equalisation and reorganisation of income.

So the Labour movement has a choice either of continuing to drift meekly with international capitalism and weakly attempt to moderate or minimise the human consequences of predatory economic imperialism by a mixture of tax adjustment and largely cosmetic job creation schemes, or of establishing an alternative structure of full, equitable employment for all the population, other than children and the severely disabled. The creation of full employment is as much a social as an economic objective.

The Government needs to get more actively into the business of expanding work of both a productive and social nature, relating public ownership plans to a policy of full employment, laying down guidelines for work opportunities for women, pensioners and disabled people, together with the supportive services, like day nurseries, which may be required, identifying meaningless or stultifying types of employment which ought to be phased out, and improving the conditions, hours and quality of work. Society has for generations accepted a responsibility for defining the minimum amenities of the home, but apart from a narrow responsibility for health and safety in factories and offices, has not yet accepted a responsibility for defining the minimum amenities of work.

There are various routes to the exercise of a more coherent employment policy. One is to set up a powerful standing Committee of Cabinet; another to establish a standing Full Employment Commission to work out the principles and objectives decided by the Government and especially briefs passed to it by the standing Committee. The scope of work of Manpower Services Commission is too restricted. In Sweden for example, from 1974 when a Royal Commission on long term employment policy was set up, a whole cluster of measures were adopted – location policies to assist industrial development in areas where employment was declining, removal and starting grants, labour market training, improved opportunities for women. The Swedish employed population, unlike most European countries, has gone on increasing and at a time of world recession counter-active measures to keep down the unemployment rate have been successful. *(Employment Tomorrow: Terms of Reference for the Royal Commission on Long Term Employment,* Ministry of Labour, Stockholm). Allowing for differences in size the Swedish Government announced a package earlier this year which would have amounted to more than a £1000m in British terms "to safeguard full employment" (Ministry of Labour, 27th January, 1977). In all the Nordic countries labour market policies have been far more positive during 1975-77, and important *independently* of economic management, than in Britain. Measures included have been the bringing forward of public investments and public orders to industry, stockpiling support, support for training instead of lay-offs and dismissals, new recruitment in the public sector and temporary employment in relief work projects in both industry and the service sector. *(Labour Market Policy in the Nordic Countries During the Recession of 1975-76,* Report of the Nordic Labour Market Committee following a meeting in Oslo in September 1976).

A major new full employment policy, and not only the adoption of an alternative economic strategy, is required in Britain. The Government's contribution has been small and has been limited to the Temporary Employment Subsidy, the Job Creation Programme, the Job Release Scheme, the Work Experience Scheme and the Youth Employment Subsidy. None of the measures make any contribution to the long-term number of jobs and are short-term palliatives. The Job Release and Youth Employment schemes are just methods of redistributing jobs from older to younger workers. In the summer the Secretary of State for Employment announced the next stages of the job creation programme. In various forms this had existed in Canada (the Canadian Local Initiatives Program), the United States, Denmark, the Netherlands and elsewhere before being introduced in Britain in 1975. From April 1978 job creation for those over 18 in its present form will cease and two separate schemes will take its place. One will offer 8,000 jobs (for a maximum of one year) to supervisors of young peoples' work experience schemes. The other is the Special Temporary Employment Programme, for people between 19 and 24 and those over 24 who have been unemployed for more than one year. The total cost is £68m. a year and is not designed to provide jobs for more than 25,000 – or less than 2 per cent of the present number of unemployed.

The persistence of the official unemployment rate over 1½ million has created large-scale misery and poverty. The rising proportion of long-term unemployed means that living standards continue to worsen. Contrary to much supposition the net incomes of unemployed people and their families are far below those at work. The evidence for last year was that the average unemployed man with wife and two children received in national insurance and supplementary benefit an income of 45 per cent of the average employed man with wife and two children. The percentage is lower still for single people and married couples without dependants. The proportion of unemployed people drawing unemployment insurance benefit has been falling and the proportion drawing earnings-related has remained small. There is no long-term rate for the unemployed receiving supplementary benefit. Few unemployed families receive exceptional circumstances additions. Unemployment insurance benefit ceases after one year. In each of these respects the living standards of unemployed people deserve further protection.

Yet it is paradoxical to pay out so many cash benefits when the creation of long-term jobs would cost little more in the short-run and represent a saving in the long run. In November 1977 the ordinary rate of supplementary benefit for a married couple was £23.80. Rent would take that amount to over £30 on average. The gap between figures like this and minimum earnings is not large and the price of not filling it by creative jobs – in lost production and poorer services as well as poverty and despair – could be very large. The Government expects a high rate of unemployment to continue into the 1980s. Instead of using that rate to damp down home demand and hence the cost of imports the Government should be devising policies to encourage self-sufficient production in substitution of imports and simultaneously reduce unemployment and the balance of payments deficit. A positive employment policy, including employment in new public industrial enterprise and more employment in public services, is a necessary part of an alternative economic strategy – and could even reduce some of the severe effects of existing economic strategy. The Government is condoning long-term mass unemployment and condoning greater and greater inequalities among the employed. In both respects the Labour movement must be awakened to action.

# 3 A Rake's Progress

**John Hughes**

John Hughes is Vice-Principal of Ruskin College, Oxford, and founder of the Trade Union Research Unit.

In September 1973 there was a total of 526,900 registered as unemployed in Great Britain; 13,000 of these were school leavers. Four years later, in September 1977, the total had reached 1,541,800, *an increase of over one million;* of these 166,200 were school leavers.

This essay seeks to identify some of the main stages by which this massive increase in unemployment came about. In the middle of the period covered, in 1975, there was the severest manufacturing recession experienced since the war. Yet in the autumn of 1977 unemployment stands some 400,000 higher than it did two years earlier at the bottom of that depression of manufacturing industry. Much of this further and most recent deterioration can be attributed to the lurch of government policy to cuts and constraints on public expenditure, and to other measures to curtail the financial deficit of the public sector.

A separate chapter examines in more detail the disproportionate burden of unemployment borne by young workers. This paper draws attention to two other dimensions of the disproportions involved in the return of mass unemployment. Between the autumn of 1973 and the autumn of 1977 male unemployment rose nearly two and a half times. *Female* unemployment rose over five-fold. Indeed, since the end of 1975 female unemployment had risen more than male unemployment in sheer numbers (a rise of over 200,000, compared with a rise of around 175,000 for males). *Regional* unemployment has also had some unusual features, notably a more severe deterioration in western regions of the economy.

Much of the material for this note was

published in a succession of Trade Union Research Unit papers from 1975 onwards.

*Employment in the 1975 Recession*

Between the second quarter of 1974 and the second quarter of 1975 manufacturing output fell by nearly 10 per cent. Comparing the two mid years, unemployment rose by over 300,000 (to 861,000 in Great Britain in June 1975, on a seasonally adjusted basis).

In fact what was surprising was the relatively moderate scale of the unemployment rise. For the age structure of the population meant that the number of employees in the economy was rising quite fast while the number of manufacturing jobs was falling steeply. In the year to mid 1975 official estimates show a rise of over 200,000 in the number of employees (an increase of over 100,000 for both male and female workers). And over the same period the number of workers employed in manufacturing industries fell by over 370,000 (or by around 5 per cent). (Working hours also fell – by about 3 per cent – in manufacturing, or the job loss would have been even more severe.)

In terms of reduced employment, the following sectors of manufacturing were hardest hit in the first stage of the recession to mid 1975:

**Table 3.I: Employment Fall by Industrial Sector**

| *% employment fall* | *sectors affected* | *actual job shrinkage* |
|---|---|---|
| 10% (approx.) | Textiles<br>Footwear | 60,000 |
| 8% (approx.) | Electrical Engineering<br>Motor Vehicles<br>Bricks etc.<br>'Other' manufacturing | 150,000 |

It was in fact a substantial increase in public sector employment that came to the rescue and limited the rise in unemployment. Between mid 1974 and mid 1975 almost 250,000 additional jobs were provided in the following sectors:

**Table 3.II: Employment Increase by Service Sector**

| *sector* | *job increases* |
|---|---|
| medical and dental services | + 88,000 employed |
| educational services | + 83,000 employed |
| public administration | + 57,000 employed |
| public transport | + 18,000 employed |

Moreover, over two thirds of these additional public sector jobs were for female workers. The loss of jobs in manufacturing had been disproportionately severe for women workers (over 180,000, nearly an 8 per cent reduction), so the creation of more public sector employment for women was of particular significance.

In this first stage of deepening unemployment, then, the main feature to note was an "offsetting" process of additional public sector job creation. It looked as if the orthodox Keynesian approach was being adopted; without it, unemployment would have climbed above one million early in 1975.

### *1975-76: Why Unemployment Worsened*

From the autumn of 1975 manufacturing output slowly recovered and by mid 1976 had improved by over 3 per cent. Instead of this bringing any relief to unemployment, the rate of increase of unemployment actually accelerated and in Great Britain rose by around 350,000 in the year to mid 1976. By autumn 1976 the seasonally adjusted rate had reached one and a quarter million (but there were in addition over 100,000 unemployed school leavers).

This further deterioration in unemployment had been widely expected; in fact the Trade Union Research Unit forecasts made late in 1975 had expected a slightly worse outturn. It is still not possible to quantify all the factors involved with precision, since official employment data for 1976 are still labelled as "provisional", but the main patterns are clear enough.

Firstly, manufacturing shed a further 200,000 jobs (thus reducing employment by nearly 600,000 in the two years to mid 1976). This was only repeating the experience of earlier trade cycles (on the basis of which, TURU had forecast a reduction of a further quarter of a million jobs in 1975-76). Rationalisation and constraints on recruitment led to a rise in labour productivity of around 6 per cent (which was modest compared with that in the same period in the previous trade cycle).

Secondly, the labour force seeking work continued to increase – though by only around 130,000. Not surprisingly, the problem of unemployment associated with this was especially severe in the younger age groups entering the labour market.

Thirdly, the constraints on real purchasing power held back employment in the private service sector (distributive trade employment fell).

Fourthly, the tighter constraints on public expenditure slowed down the increase in public service employment (thus educational and medical services increased employment by around 70,000, about 100,000 less than in the year before). TURU had assumed an even more abrupt check to employment in this sector.

Fifthly, employment in construction continued to contract – as it had done every year since 1973 – in face of cut backs in physical investment by private sector industries and services.

### *1976-77: Recent Trends in Unemployment*

At the time of the April 1976 Budget the government was projecting – on the basis of large scale deficit financing, and the pay/tax reduction trade-off of the second stage of the "social contract" – a renewal of economic growth at up to 4 per cent per annum.

In fact, in the face of increasing difficulties of exchange rate and monetary management, the government retreated towards a more and more restrictive approach to national economic management. Its peculiar combination of increased indirect taxation (and steep rises in nationalised industry prices), and cuts in public expenditure combined to reduce the rate of economic growth to a mere 1 per cent per annum. Both through the severity of the fall in real personal living standards arising from its policies, and through the severe "cash limits" constraints on public services, its policies blocked any improvement in employment.

The provisional employment figures for mid 1976 to mid 1977 indicate a modest rise of around 100,000 in employment in manufacturing industries, but a small net reduction in employment in all other sectors of the economy.

The increased employment in manufacturing is perhaps not very securely based. It is most noticeable in vehicles (where production has been adversely affected by industrial disputes) more thinly in other sectors in engineering, the food industries, and clothing. One reason why it is not possible to "read off" likely employment figures in manufacturing by looking at output data is that the greatly increased incidence of industrial disputes (mostly "unofficial") in 1977 has taken its toll of output in a wide range of industries. But it is clear also that more severe competitive pressures are developing (later in 1977) in important sectors such as steel and chemicals.

The continued rise in unemployment in 1977 is associated, not simply with the very limited increase in total employment, but once again with a rise in the number of employees (at work or unemployed). From mid 1976 to mid 1977 this increase in the labour force consists entirely of a rise of some 150,000 in the number of females in the labour forces (with no change in the number of males).

Consequently the marked rise in women's unemployment is being fed from two sources. Firstly the continued rise in the number of girls and women in the labour force (in the *two* years to mid 1977 an addition of over 230,000, compared with only 50,000 males). Secondly the choking off of the rise in employment outside manufacturing, partly because of the depression of private service job opportunities in face of falling real personal incomes since 1975, partly because of the increasingly severe constraints on employment in the public services. The number of female employees at work in manufacturing has still not regained its 1975 level (let alone the much higher 1974 level) even if it is now rising slowly. But the educational and health services provide between them more jobs for female workers than all the manufacturing industries put together, and in those sectors the limits on public spending have brought the secular expansion of employment grinding to a halt.

The outcome has been a doubling of *registered* unemployment of female workers in the two years to September 1977 (to reach 380,000 seasonally adjusted). In actual numbers, female unemployment has consistently grown faster than male unemployment through 1976 and 1977. The information now available on young workers shows quite clearly the continuing and disproportionate deterioration of the labour market situation of girls and young women workers. This is not in any obvious sense capitalism's retort to the achievement of "equal pay" (if only because pay is still far from equal); it is rather more social democracy's lurch back towards monetarism and pre-Keynesian orthodoxies. It is above all the combination of real reductions in public service expenditure together with reductions in real personal disposable income that for the whole period of 1976 and 1977 has blocked any changes for the better in the labour market and has enlarged the "reserve army" of unemployed labour.

It is important therefore to emphasise once again the economic rationality of a change in stance on public expenditure, and the strength of the case for a selective expansion in public service spending and associated increases in employment. There is even considerable scope for this within the expenditure figures and size of public financial deficit that were budgeted for (and agreed with the IMF). This arises from persistent under-spending of "cash limits", and from substantial reductions in interest rates. The fall in interest rates is particularly important for the budgets of local authorities; thus, whereas the interest rates on 3 months deposits with local authorities were around 15 per cent in the fourth quarter of 1976 they were down to 8 per cent as early as the second quarter of 1977 and have been even lower since.

Unfortunately given the stance of the Treasury (both before and after the autumn "budget" of 1977) and of Conservative local authorities, little of this potential for employment creating expenditure is being used. Yet in terms of real "social opportunity costs" (what the community has to give up in order to have the benefits of the additional spending) the cost of additional public spending of a labour intensive character has never been lower:

– the import content is low, and the state of the balance of payments is not a constraint;

– resource costs are low since under-employed capacity is prevalent; this is not only true of much of the private sector (such as building and construction) which would benefit from public sector orders, but in the public sector as well there is much under-used social capital; consequently re-employment of under-employed capital and unemployed workers would not displace resources from productive activity in other sectors (least of all if increased public expenditure were selectively aimed at the worst sectors of under- and un-employment);

– exchequer costs are low; re-employment would offer substantial savings on unemployment and other social benefits and would generate a revenue inflow from additional incomes; borrowing costs are low; the *relative* costs of labour intensive services has been falling since 1975.

Consequently, with increasing irrationality, the deflation of both public services and private demand[1] in 1977 has meant that as the summer bulge of new entrants joined the labour force a further damaging increase in unemployment came through. After expansionary and contracting forces cancelling out and leading to near stability in the (seasonally adjusted) unemployment level from autumn of 1976 to May of 1977, we have had the surge of unemployment as set out in Table 3.III. Perhaps it should be pointed out that these disturbing figures – with a rise of over 125,000 in unemployment in only four months – owe nothing to the number of jobless school leavers, as these are excluded from the figures. (For the record there were 142,000 jobless school

1 Consumer demand has been held back more than the government consciously sought. The pressures of government pay policies and "guidelines" and the arguments over the TUC's "twelve month rule" have meant that millions of workers have failed to settle pay changes by their due date; since June 1977 each month's figures have shown at least 3 million fewer workers settling in 1977 than in the corresponding months of 1976. Assuming that settlements when finally made will be backdated, there will be a catching up of purchasing power and demand in late 1977 and in early 1978.

**Table 3.III: Unemployment Trends: Year to September 1977**

*(Great Britain. Seasonally adjusted)*

| | *Total 1000's* | *Male 1000's* | *Female 1000's* |
|---|---|---|---|
| September 1976 | 1265.7 | 957.6 | 308.1 |
| May 1977 | 1262.1 | 943.8 | 318.3 |
| September 1977 | 1388.7 | 1008.6 | 380.1 |
| *Percentage Change* | | | |
| September 1976/Sept. 1977 | + 9.7% | + 5.3% | +23.4% |
| September 1976/May 1977 | – 0.3% | – 1.4% | + 3.3% |
| May 1977/Sept. 1977 | +10.0% | + 6.9% | +19.4% |

*Source:* Department of Employment Gazette.

leavers in September 1976 and 166,000 in September 1977; the number of registered unemployed school leavers actually rose by 124,000 between May and September 1977.)

### *The Regional Dimension*

Official analyses seem to treat the regional dimension of unemployment as of diminishing significance. This is not the case. Over the period since 1973 all regions have suffered a heavy increase in unemployment rates; but the figures have also shown fairly persistently a more serious deterioration in the western regions of Great Britain. The most recent data show a further worsening of unemployment in these western regions and in the northern regions of the economy as well.

Table 3.IV compares the unemployment rates in the regions in July 1973 and in July 1977, and shows the *increase* in unemployment as a percentage of the total labour force in each region over those four years. The regions are listed in order of the *severity of increase* in the unemployment rate. The final column simply records the level of unemployment in each region in thousands in July 1977; it is, after all, important to grasp that although the South East region has the lowest unemployment rate it accounted in July 1977 for a quarter of the registered unemployment in Great Britain.

The pattern of unemployment that is revealed will need closer study in the future. The more severe increase in unemployment in the western regions may represent a locational shift stimulated both by EEC membership and the development encouraged by North Sea oil. It may also reflect the weakness of regional economies whose plants are often branches of enterprises whose main base lies elsewhere (this is a problem for Wales and the South West).

**Table 3.IV: Regional Unemployment as a % of total employees: 1973 to 1977**

| *(Seasonally adjusted)* | *July 1973* % | *July 1977* % | *Increase, '73 to '77* % | *July 1977 in 1000's* |
|---|---|---|---|---|
| Wales | 3.4 | 7.6 | + 4.2 | 79.4 |
| South West | 2.4 | 6.6 | + 4.2 | 105.4 |
| North West | 3.4 | 7.0 | + 3.6 | 198.1 |
| W. Midlands | 2.1 | 5.6 | + 3.5 | 127.5 |
| Scotland | 4.4 | 7.8 | + 3.4 | 170.0 |
| East Anglia | 1.9 | 5.3 | + 3.4 | 36.4 |
| Northern | 4.5 | 7.8 | + 3.3 | 105.0 |
| E. Midlands | 2.0 | 5.0 | + 3.0 | 76.2 |
| South East | 1.5 | 4.5 | + 3.0 | 335.9 |
| Yorks. & Humb. | 2.8 | 5.5 | + 2.7 | 113.9 |

*(Figures exclude unemployed school leavers.)*

*Source:* Dept. of Employment Gazette

Nor do the latest developments in employment suggest any diminution in regional employment differences; on the contrary. By November 1977 the provisional figures show a further rise since July of 0.5 per cent in the unemployment rate in Wales and the Northern region, and of 0.3 per cent in the South West, North West, and in Scotland. By contrast the unemployment rate in the South East has fallen slightly. This is in fact the classic pattern of the early stages of a cyclical "recovery".

### *A Comment*

It should not be thought that the shift to mass unemployment that disfigures the British economy is so very different to that in other major industrial economies, especially those with problems of structural adjustment to intensified and more dynamic competition. The following general characteristics are worthy of note:

- The major economies have emerged from the 1975 recession with somewhere near 10 per cent under-utilisation of their "productive potential" persisting.
- The controlling groups in these countries are reluctant to "manage" a rapid expansion of industrial output. Such an expansion by *most* major countries would be expected to trigger violent increases in primary product prices. The contradiction is that slow growth is limiting the readiness to invest in additional capacity for primary products, so laying up further problems for the future. Expansion by a single country, given the openness of most of them, would be seen as leading to powerful adverse swings in the balance of payments.

– Much of the industrial investment that is occurring is aimed at cost reduction (to improve competitiveness) and reduces labour requirements, or at capital intensive development of fuel and power capacity (including nuclear).
– This does not suggest that the internationally competitive sector of modern economies can directly generate additional employment to mop up the persistent structural unemployment that has emerged.
– However, constraints on real personal income caused by under-employment of capacity and worsened "terms of trade" (e.g. vis-a-vis oil) have reduced the scope for expansion of employment in private sector services and local industries.
– Most countries, not only the UK, have curtailed public expenditure programmes in face of mounting deficits in public sector finance. (Up to the mid 1970s the growth of public sectors had been generally an important source of additional job opportunities.)
– A number of countries have an age structure which is leading to a substantial increase in the number of young workers entering the labour market; high rates of unemployment among workers under 25 are general.

In these circumstances the unemployment problem cannot be dealt with solely by conventional "growth" led by the commercial sector. In British terms it will not emerge that a by-product of the "industrial strategy" is an enlargement of employment. Major inroads into unemployment by the early 1980s would require:

i. A sustained programme of increased public service expenditure; the political and economic problems of managing the renewed growth of public spending have to be faced.
ii. Reduction in total labour supply through work sharing, including shorter working hours, re-manning to allow for planned replacement of staff on an increased number of "rest" days, etc.
iii. Particular measures to assist younger workers through programmes combining job and "work experience" opportunities with improved training and further education.
iv. The renewed growth of real personal incomes.
v. A strengthening of the internationally competitive sector of the economy, both public (e.g. steel; motors, oil; aero-space; shipbuilding, etc.) and private. This is a necessary condition for economic policies aimed at full employment, even though on its own it is not a sufficient condition.

The easing of balance of payments pressures on the UK economy through the development of oil production, and the greater flexibility this also provides for the handling of public sector finance, make more readily achievable a radical programme to eliminate large scale unemployment. But this would still only represent a part of the wider international planning of development and employment creation that is required.

# PART TWO

## The Impact on Special Groups

# 4 Young Workers

John Hughes

Mass unemployment of young workers in Britain emerged as a new phenomenon in 1975 and has persisted, and indeed substantially worsened, since then. As it appeared in the context of the industrial recession of 1975 it was at first thought that it would fall away rapidly once renewed expansion of the economy developed. Not only has there been the most hesitant of all postwar recoveries from recession; it is now clear that the employment problem of young workers is so severe to be treated as "structural" for some years to come. What is needed is not the temporary palliatives of a contra-cyclical approach but a bold and planned change in the nature of the labour market as experienced by young workers.

The mass unemployment of young workers that has emerged in Britain is an experience shared with other countries. Indeed, the appearance of extensive unemployment in Britain among young workers in 1971-72 was only swept away by the coincidental timing of ROSLA (the raising of the school leaving age) which withheld a whole year's cohort of young workers from the labour market in 1973. The experience of disproportionate unemployment among the young had emerged earlier in the economies of the USA, Canada, and Italy. What we now have is a remarkable similarity as between the economies of the UK, and of North America, and of many European countries, notably Italy and France. The OECD's statistics tell the tale: (see Table 4.I).

Thus by 1976, the unemployment rates among the under 25s were in the 12 per cent to 14 per cent range in most of these countries (including Britain) compared with unemployment rates centring

**Table 4.I: Unemployment rates by age in seven major countries**
*Per cent of civilian labour force; figures in brackets are the percentage of total unemployment*

| | *1973* | | *1974* | | *1975* | | *1976* | |
|---|---|---|---|---|---|---|---|---|
| | *Under 25 yrs. of age* | *Over 25 yrs. of age* | *Under 25 yrs. of age* | *Over 25 yrs. of age* | *Under 25 yrs. of age* | *Over 25 yrs. of age* | *Under 25 yrs. of age* | *Over 25 yrs. of age* |
| U.S. | 10.5 | 3.1 | 11.8 | 3.6 | 16.1 | 6.0 | 14.4 | 5.5 |
| | (51) | (49) | (51) | (49) | (46) | (54) | (46) | (54) |
| Japan | 2.4 | 1.0 | 2.5 | 1.2 | 3.1 | 1.7 | 3.0 | 1.8 |
| | (34) | (66) | (30) | (70) | (25) | (75) | (23) | (77) |
| Germany | 1.0 | 1.0 | 3.1 | 2.0 | 5.8 | 3.7 | 5.3 | 3.8 |
| | (19) | (81) | (27) | (73) | (27) | (73) | (24) | (76) |
| France | 3.2 | 1.7 | 4.3 | 1.7 | 7.6 | 2.8 | 8.0 | 3.2 |
| | (35) | (65) | (40) | (60) | (42) | (58) | (40) | (60) |
| United Kingdom | 2.9 | 2.0 | 3.4 | 2.0 | 8.6 | 2.9 | 12.0 | 3.8 |
| | (28) | (72) | (30) | (70) | (42) | (58) | (44) | (56) |
| Italy | 12.6 | 1.6 | 11.1 | 1.2 | 12.8 | 1.5 | 14.3 | 1.6 |
| | (63) | (37) | (65) | (35) | (64) | (36) | (64) | (36) |
| Canada | 9.7 | 3.5 | 9.4 | 3.3 | 12.1 | 4.3 | 12.8 | 4.2 |
| | (48) | (52) | (49) | (51) | (47) | (53) | (48) | (52) |

*Source:* OECD: Economic Outlook, July 1977

around 4 per cent for the older age groups. In the UK, North America, and France, the young unemployed accounted for over 40 per cent of the total, in Italy over 60 per cent of the total. Moreover the same OECD report which carried these figures points out that "except in North America there does not seem to have been important re-entrance into the work-force in the recovery period. This is in marked contrast to previous cyclical experience".

The British experience of unemployment of young workers needs to be examined in more detail. The following are the salient points:

a. Age and duration of unemployment data are available every six months, for January and for July. The latest such information is therefore for July 1977. In terms, first of all, of overall numbers, there were at the last count 708,000 registered as unemployed under 25 years of age. This total was made up of 404,000 young males, and 304,000 females under 25. At the same date, unemployment in the *older* age groups (25+) totalled 603,000 for men and only 162,000 for women.

b. The July totals are swollen by the large number of school leavers included, 241,600 in all. It should be noted that this leaves still the enormous residual figure of 467,000 unemployed under 25 *excluding* school leavers. The school leaver problem has worsened dramatically since 1974:

**Table 4.II: Unemployed School leavers: 1974 to 1977**

| | *1974* *1000's* | *1975* *1000's* | *1976* *1000's* | *1977* *1000's* |
|---|---|---|---|---|
| June | 5.4 | 18.4 | 118.2 | 142.7 |
| July | 14.4 | 55.3 | 199.4 | 241.6 |
| August | 56.0 | 158.2 | 194.5 | 220.4 |
| September | 33.4 | 117.9 | 142.3 | 166.2 |

c. Not till 1977 did official government sources offer estimates of the percentage unemployment rate by age group, although the Trade Union Research Unit had produced its own estimates. The official estimates are worth giving in full: (see Table 4.III).

Among the salient features of these figures are the greater deterioration in the unemployment rates for young female workers, and the fact that at the seasonal peak (July) the unemployment rate of the 16-17 year olds has moved up from around one in eight in 1975 to one in four in 1976 and to nearly 30 per cent in 1977. Double figure unemployment rates for young male workers under 25 are also clearly in evidence.

d. What these figures still do not do is to bring out the greatly increased severity of longer period unemployment among the young. Taking the figures for those unemployed over 13 weeks (i.e. over three months): (See Table 4:IV).

To look more closely at the July 1977 information. The most severe incidence of longer period unemployment was in the age group 20-24, with 124,000 unemployed for over 13 weeks (and of those 80,000 unemployed for over six months). The longer period unemployment of this age group is the worst of any such five year age group as far as women workers are concerned, and for male workers it is only exceeded in the 60-64 age group.

e. All of this is despite the numbers covered by special employment and training schemes. These must have been keeping over 100,000 young workers at any one time off the register.

*Special Schemes*

At this point it is useful to comment on the government's response in the form of special schemes.

**Table 4.III: Unemployment rates by age**
**Estimated unemployment rates by age, Great Britain**

*Percentages*

| | *July 1975* | *Jan. 1976* | *July 1976* | *Jan. 1977* | *July 1977* |
|---|---|---|---|---|---|
| *Males* | | | | | |
| 16-17 | 13.8 | 12.3 | 26.7 | 12.8 | 28.6 |
| 18-19 | 9.6 | 11.2 | 10.7 | 11.1 | 11.4 |
| 20-24 | 6.8 | 10.0 | 9.3 | 10.1 | 9.7 |
| 25-29 | 5.2 | 7.0 | 6.6 | 7.3 | 6.7 |
| 30-39 | 4.4 | 5.9 | 5.6 | 6.3 | 6.0 |
| 40-49 | 3.7 | 4.8 | 4.6 | 5.1 | 4.8 |
| 50-59 | 3.7 | 4.7 | 4.6 | 5.1 | 4.9 |
| 60 and over | 7.8 | 9.1 | 9.1 | 9.5 | 8.7 |
| All ages | 5.4 | 6.9 | 7.2 | 7.2 | 7.5 |
| *Females* | | | | | |
| 16-17 | 10.4 | 12.0 | 25.6 | 14.1 | 29.6 |
| 18-19 | 6.1 | 8.1 | 9.2 | 9.9 | 11.2 |
| 20-24 | 3.1 | 5.3 | 5.9 | 7.0 | 7.6 |
| 25-29 | 2.1 | 3.1 | 3.5 | 4.4 | 4.6 |
| 30-39 | 1.0 | 1.5 | 1.8 | 2.2 | 2.3 |
| 40-49 | 0.9 | 1.2 | 1.4 | 1.7 | 1.8 |
| 50-59 | 1.3 | 1.7 | 1.9 | 2.2 | 2.2 |
| 60 and over | 0.2 | 0.2 | 0.2 | 0.2 | 0.2 |
| All ages | 2.1 | 2.9 | 4.0 | 3.8 | 4.9 |
| *Total* | | | | | |
| 16-17 | 12.1 | 12.1 | 26.2 | 13.3 | 29.1 |
| 18-19 | 8.0 | 9.8 | 10.0 | 10.6 | 11.3 |
| 20-24 | 5.2 | 8.0 | 7.9 | 8.9 | 8.8 |
| 25-29 | 4.2 | 5.7 | 5.6 | 6.3 | 6.0 |
| 30-39 | 3.1 | 4.2 | 4.1 | 4.7 | 4.6 |
| 40-49 | 2.5 | 3.3 | 3.3 | 3.6 | 3.5 |
| 50-59 | 2.7 | 3.5 | 3.5 | 3.9 | 3.8 |
| 60 and over | 5.5 | 6.4 | 6.4 | 6.7 | 6.2 |
| All ages | 4.1 | 5.3 | 5.9 | 5.8 | 6.5 |

*Source:* Department of Employment Gazette: October 1977.

**Table 4.IV: Under 25s Unemployed over 13 weeks**

| | |
|---|---|
| July 1975 | 102,000 |
| July 1976 | 190,000 |
| July 1977 | 225,000 |

*16-18 age group.* In July 1977 the government announced that it was developing additional measures based on the Holland Report of the MSC (Manpower Services Commission). The new programme integrates a series of measures aimed at training and work experience provision for the 16-18 group. In scale the objective is to double the provision under earlier schemes to build up by autumn 1978 to a maximum of 130,000 places on the programme. It hardly looks as if the enhanced programme for winter 1977/78 will do more than keep pace with the higher level of unemployment. In the winter of 1976/77 there were over 180,000 unemployed in this age range (and about 60,000 being helped by the then existing programmes); in the winter of 1977/78 there may be about 175,000 unemployed (and a further 100,000 being given training and work experience at any one time). By winter 1978/79 there may be as many being helped by the programme as remain unemployed; it is still some way from creating a full range of training or job opportunities.

One important and welcome part of the government's new programme is to concentrate on the most disadvantaged (this contrasts with earlier styles of training provision and selection):

> "We intend that places should go only to those young people who have been unemployed for at least six weeks, and the emphasis will be on those who are the least qualified, with the poorest employment prospects." (Department of Employment Gazette, July 1977, p.690.)

*19-24 age group.* The approach here is far less adequate. The main programme of temporary employment particularly aimed at this age group has been JCP (Job Creation Programme). The most recent figure of the number covered is only 44,000, but well over half of these could be expected to have been in the 19-24 age range.

The replacement programme has a name, STEP (Special Temporary Employment Programme) and is to "build up" to 25,000 places concentrated in areas of exceptionally severe unemployment. This is quite noticeably less than the current level of JCP and the government gloss that "priority will be given to maintaining the number of places currently provided under JCP for the 19-24 age group" can only be interpreted as a cover up for decline in provision. Support for this age group is clearly taking a STEP backwards and it is to be hoped that the trade union representatives on the MSC will fight for a much stronger programme. At the July count there were nearly one third of a million unemployed in the 19-24 age range.

### *Why "Structural"?*

On the supply side, the "age bulge" presents growing cohorts of young workers to the labour market. The number of 16 year olds in the population is expected to rise from 826,000 in 1976 to 923,000 in 1981 and only decline thereafter. School leavers "available for employment" are already at the high level of 650,000 p.a. and this figure is rising towards 700,000. In addition there are increasing numbers entering the labour market for the first time from higher education.

It is important to recall the earlier pattern of entry of the least educationally qualified into the labour market. A third entered jobs involving negligible training. A disproportionately high ratio of the girls (26 per cent in 1974) went into distribution. So did a disproportionate number of boys (15 per cent) and there was an equivalent entry by boys into construction trades (also 15 per cent of 16-17 year old leavers). Clearly such job opportunities are restricted by the sustained contraction of the building and construction industry, and the lack of expansion in employment in distribution.

The least qualified entrants must be adversely affected by the long period decline in demand for manual labour (thus the "input" of manual labour measures in total hours in manufacturing has fallen by one quarter since the early 1960s). Young unqualified males in regions where manual work still predominates are facing a labour market with dwindling requirement for manual workers and characterised by persistently high unemployment rates for manual male workers. Since 1974 *total* employment – manual and non-manual – in manufacturing has fallen by nearly 500,000 and on earlier cyclical experience is unlikely to recoup more than a small part of such job loss.

Young workers are also exposed to the "planning" of recruitment, and least covered by the build up of job rights of older workers. Controlling and limiting recruitment to avoid the need for large scale redundancies has been the way to manage falling labour requirements with least risk of resistance by organised labour. "Seniority" is least available to young workers, whether by industrial agreements or legislation.

### *What is to be done?*

The major expansion of a linked training and work experience programme aimed primarily at the age groups up to 18 is coming some two years later than it should. It is also *not* being adequately supported by additional finance to strengthen further educational provision and the development of sixth form colleges within the comprehensive school system. The school system has still not been required to break down the rigidity of its approach which is built round full time education both before and after 16. There would be considerable advantages from linking periods of "work experience" (properly monitored) with periods of continuing school education (whether on a "block" or part-time basis); such flexibility does not have to be the exclusive prerogative of the further education sector.

This paper has already made clear the failure of the government to develop a stronger programme of job creation to help the massive unemployment of the 19-24 year age group. The shape of such a programme has not even been considered seriously. The key to it would have to be a rapid development of expenditure and recruitment on a wide range of (selective) public service and public industrial activity. Of course, such schemes would not be exclusively aimed at a particular age-group; but they could be concentrated in areas of high unemployment and linked with further training schemes. The emphasis should shift as rapidly as possible from "temporary" schemes to permanent work, and the public sector's trade unions should be closely involved in the organisation of effective schemes to improve public services and create worthwhile jobs.

Beyond this, the solution of the problems of younger workers connects with wider and more general issues such as the scope for planned "work sharing", and the re-location of some of the job creation of the finance sector of the economy (over-concentrated in the South East).

# 5 The Poor*

**Frank Field**

Frank Field is Director of the Child Poverty Action Group and the Low Pay Unit.

"Economists and top policy makers debate the question: how much unemployment can society stand? Strictly speaking, it is not the country that is being asked to stand unemployment. Unemployment does not, like . . . God's gentle rain, fall uniformly upon everyone . . . It strikes from the underneath and it strikes particularly at those at the bottom of society."
– (E. Liebow, "No Man can live with the terrible knowledge that he is not needed", *New York Magazine*, 5 April 1970).

If unemployment doesn't fall like God's gentle rain, who has been most affected by the record post war unemployment? The first part of this paper shows that unemployment has struck hardest at the youngest and oldest members of the labour market, has fallen more heavily on some regions of the country than others, and is more heavily concentrated amongst the unskilled and semi-skilled workers.

*Age Differences*

The two groups at whom unemployment strikes most heavily are those below 25 years and workers over 55. During 1976 800,000 young people under 25 were unemployed at one time or another. And while those under 25 make up 20% of the labour force, they now comprise over 40% of the unemployed. *Youthaid,* the national youth employment initiative, estimates that in several parts of the country, including the centres of our cities, as many as one in four young people is unemployed. In the black spots the per-

**This chapter is based on material from* The Conscript Army: a study of Britain's unemployed, *edited by the author and published by Routledge & Kegan Paul. The author would like to thank Louise Burghes for her help.*

centage is even higher. A survey commissioned for the MSC's Holland Report showed that 30% of young people aged 16 to 19 are unemployed in Central Liverpool.

As well as being one of the groups bearing the brunt of present unemployment, many young people in work are to be found in the most marginal occupations. There is now considerable evidence to suggest that in some areas there is a large turnover of young workers particularly those offered "dead end" jobs. For example, in one Northern city there was found to "be a 'core' of boys who do not stay in any job for a long period of time and who lose jobs frequently." (D. Phillips, "Young and Unemployed in a Northern City", in D. Weir [ed.] *Men in Work in Modern Society,* Fontana 1973.)

Older workers are also overrepresented amongst the unemployed. Over the last ten years men aged between 60 and 64 have been about 8% of the labour force; but their unemployment rate has always been twice as high and sometimes over 20%. In addition the manpower services Commission suggests that "there are plausible general grounds for thinking that the 'young' and the 'old' . . . because of their age will be further disadvantaged in regions where joblessness is generally high." (S. Mukherjee, *There's work to be done,* HMSO, 1974, p.52.)

### *Regional Inequality*

Any set of national figures masks significant regional differences in the incidence of unemployment. At present unemployment stands at a post-war record; the average for the whole country is 5.9% (UK April 1977). But we can see from Table 3.IV. the regional differences that this average figure masks. But even these figures underestimate the impact of unemployment, for the hardest hit areas have a smaller proportion of working age in the labour force. Also the likelihood is workers are unemployed for a longer period of time in areas where there is high unemployment.

### *Class differences*

Unemployment also falls more heavily on unskilled working people. Using Census information Nicholas Bosanquet and Guy Standing have shown that the rates of unemployment for white collar and professional workers are generally lower than for manual workers. The authors write: "The most striking difference is that between the rate for the unskilled – in a survey done in April 1966 at a time when the demand for labour in the economy was high – and the rates for the other groups. The unskilled rate . . . was more than twice as high as the general rate." In 1966 the general unemployment rate was 2.9%

while for the unskilled it touched 6.9%. (N. Bosanquet & Guy Standing, "Government Employment 1966 to 1970", *British Journal of Industrial Relations,* July 1972.) The authors note however that there is a significant difference in the numbers of unskilled males classified as unemployed in the Census data compared with the information from the DE. The Census for April 1966 puts the numbers of registered unskilled at about 50,000 while the DE recorded in March 1966 a total of 123,000. The authors concluded, therefore, that the estimated rate of 8.6% for labourers "may well be too low". Using the DE material they estimate, the unemployment rate for labourers "will be more than 15%".

### *Women*

It is difficult to give an accurate picture of unemployment among women because of the extent to which women do not register. What we can safely say is that the registered unemployment figures do understate the amount of unemployment among women. Nevertheless the evidence suggests that unemployment among women has been rising fast as a result of the current recession. Until the end of 1974, men outnumbered women on the register by five to one; the ratio now is three to one, perhaps because women are increasingly registering as unemployed. (Treasury, 1976)

Another way of looking at the increasing unemployment among women is to compare their share of unemployment with their share of employment. Employment among women has actually begun to fall recently but rose steadily between 1970 and 1976 from 38% to 41% of employees in employment: at the same time female unemployment has risen from 14% to 25% of total unemployment, more than trebling in absolute terms. This led the Annual Report of the Manpower Services Commission to conclude that "it is clear that female unemployment, though still at a lower level than for males, can no longer be regarded as a minor problem." (*Labour Research,* October 1976)

### *Minority Groups*

Unlike the minority population in general, women and young people from minority groups have consistently had unemployment rates higher than their general populations.

Figures from the 1971 Census (which are not distorted by the propensity of women to register) show that unemployment among women from minority groups was 9.3% in that year compared to 5.6% for women in general. Unemployment has been particularly marked among younger women. Unemployment rates have also been particularly high among young male West Indians. In 1971, the Census figures show 16.9% of young West Indian males as unemployed, twice the rate for other young economically active males at 8.6%. The high incidence of unemployment among young West Indians has been well documented elsewhere. Concern about these high levels is increased by the extent to which the official Department of Employment figures may underestimate unemployment because of non-registration. A CRC survey in 1972 suggested that about 50% of the young unemployed were not registered. (Community Relations Commission, *Unemployment and Homelessness,* 1974, Table 12, p.68)

A cursory glance at the numbers of registered disabled unemployed again shows that "unemployment does not, like . . . God's gentle rain, fall uniformly upon everybody". At the present time 14% of registered disabled are unemployed, yet only three government departments, almost no local authorities and nationalised industries and only 40% of private employers fulfilled the 3% quota. But even this percentage underestimates the proportion of unemployed disabled in the depressed regions as many of them have long since been driven out of the labour market. The same is true of course of many old workers and the Government's job swap scheme is just one example of moves to redefine away unemployment amongst those who are hit hardest.

As unemployment falls most heavily on the young and the old, hits disproportionately workers in certain areas of the country and is more heavily concentrated amongst semi and unskilled workers, one could be forgiven for thinking that the welfare state would provide a non-means-tested safety net for those who are bearing the brunt of our unemployment. A detailed look at the workings of the National Insurance scheme shows otherwise.

### *Benefits for the Unemployed*

There are three benefits for the unemployed; the flat rate unemployment benefit, the earnings related supplement and supplementary benefit. In addition a worker may qualify under the redundancy payment scheme. However, this is a payment to compensate him for loss of his job, rather than tide him over the period during which he is out of work. People who work for an employer are usually covered by unemployment benefit after the first three days of unemployment; the self-employed are excluded from this scheme. In order to qualify for unemployment benefit a claimant has to satisfy the contributions conditions and show that he is available for work.

An unemployed claimant may draw flat rate unemployment benefit for up to 312 days and, as Sundays are not included as payment days, this amounts to 12 months in any one period of interruption of employment. Once a claimant has exhausted his right to benefit he cannot qualify again for unemployment benefit until he has been back at work and paying contributions as an employed person for at least 13 weeks. The rates (November 1977) for flat rate unemployment benefit are £14.70 for a single claimant, £9.10 for a wife and £3.50 for the first and £3.00 a week for subsequent children.

A claimant may be eligible for an earnings related supplement to his flat rate unemployment benefit if he is aged 18 and over and under minimum pensionable age. This benefit entitlement runs for six months. But although claimants will have paid their full contributions, they are disallowed from drawing a full earnings related supplement if, together with the flat rate benefit, this brings their total benefit to above 85% of their average weekly earnings. Even the official definition of average weekly earnings work against many low paid for these are not their current weekly earnings. Instead a claimant's total reckonable earnings in the relevant tax year are divided by 50 and this sum can often by considerably lower than current earnings. The relevant tax year refers to the last completed financial year prior to the claim for benefit. So a claim in December 1977 will be based on earnings during the tax year April 1975 to April 1976. During 1976 61,800 unemployed claimants had this "wage stop" imposed on their benefit even though they had paid the contributions for a full earnings related benefit. (House of Lords *Hansard,* 22 December 1976, Vol.378, col.1442)

Unemployed claimants and their families who have few private resources on which to fall back may be eligible for a weekly payment from the SBC to bring their unemployment and earnings related benefit up to the state poverty line. The current benefit rates are £23.55 for a married couple, weekly benefits for children ranging from £4.10 to £8.90, plus a payment to cover the rent.

### *Stigmatising the unemployed*

A major distinction is made in the National Insurance scheme between claimants who draw long and short term benefits. The unemployed can only draw benefit for up to a year and during that time the benefit is paid at a lower rate. Long term claimants, such as the old or widowed, draw a weekly benefit of £17.50 as opposed to £14.70 if they are sick or unemployed, and £28.00 as a married couple, compared with £23.80 for those claimants who are classified as short term beneficiaries. The rates for children also vary. The first children of claimants on the higher rate attract a weekly benefit of £7.40, with payments of £6.90 for second and subsequent children in contrast to weekly allowances of £3.50 for the first and £3.00 for the other children of sick or unemployed claimants.

There is a similar distinction between so called long and short term claimants in the supplementary benefit scheme. Ever since 1966, when the Ministry of Social Security Act came into force, there has been a tiered system of benefits. When the new supplementary benefit rates became effective in November 1977 the difference between those on the long term scale rate and other claimants rose to £4.80 a week for couples and £3.40 for single persons.

The reasoning behind the long and short term scale rates is sound. Claimants who have been on benefit for any length of time are likely to have exhausted their savings and to be experiencing a severe depletion of household stocks, such as bedding, furniture, clothing and so on. What is wrong is that the distinction is misapplied for a growing number of unemployed are also long term claimants. As the unemployed are automatically excluded from the long term rate, irrespective of the time they have been on benefit, the rule helps to reinforce in the public eye the false distinction between "deserving" and "undeserving" claimants.

### *Unemployment and Poverty*

Despite the provisions of the National Insurance scheme, an increasing number of unemployed claimants are being plunged into poverty. In 1948 only 16% of the unemployed were drawing national assistance. By 1976 this had risen to 46%. But why is it that, with the provision of social security measures which, in Beveridge's phrase, were designed to prevent Want being the inevitable result of unemployment, we find an increasing pauperisation amongst the unemployed?

There are two reasons why the present national insurance scheme does not prevent poverty resulting from unemployment. The first is that not every unemployed person is covered by the scheme because either they have insufficient contributions, or they have been unemployed for a long time and have therefore exhausted their right to unemployment benefit. The second reason is that in most instances unemployment benefit is not paid at a level high enough to raise the income of those claimants who have no private resources to a level above the state poverty line.

Regularly the Government publishes data on the numbers of unemployed and the type of benefit to which they are entitled. The latest detailed breakdown shows that at any one time one in six claimants is drawing no benefit at all. Moreover, the proportion of unemployed claimants drawing national insurance benefits has been falling in recent years; from over 70% in 1948 to less than 40% in 1976. But even if a claimant is eligible for the flat rate unemployment pay, this will not automatically raise his income to a level above the state poverty line. For example, if a claimant has two children aged 7 and 12 and pays rent of £5 a week, the poverty line for himself and his family is £39.60 a week. His flat rate unemployment benefit however comes to only £30.30 (including the Child Benefit payments). And although the earnings related supplement can provide an important additional source of income for unemployed men and their families, wage related payments do not automatically guarantee that a family will have an income above the state poverty line. In May 1976 there were 31,000 claimants drawing flat rate unemployment benefit plus earnings related supplement who also qualified for a supplementary allowance. What we do not know however is the number of unemployed men drawing flat rate and wage related unemployment benefit whose income was below the state poverty line but through ignorance of their rights or for some other reason, failed to claim supplementary allowance.

Because of our failure to provide a comprehensive and generous income support system we have seen that losing one's job is still a major cause of poverty in this country. Given the current economic forecast

**Table 5.I**
**The numbers and percentage of unemployed supplementary benefit allowance claimants**

| *Year* | *Number (1,000s)* | *Percentage of all allowance cases* |
|---|---|---|
| 1960 | 128 | 24.6 |
| 1961 | 131 | 24.6 |
| 1962 | 202 | 31.8 |
| 1963 | 185 | 28.9 |
| 1964 | 131 | 22.7 |
| 1965 | 112 | 19.4 |
| 1966 | 179 | 26.5 |
| 1967 | 224 | 29.7 |
| 1968 | 220 | 28.3 |
| 1969 | 228 | 28.0 |
| 1970 | 239 | 28.6 |
| 1971 | 387 | 39.1 |
| 1972 | 392 | 39.1 |
| 1973 | 249 | 30.0 |
| 1974 | 301 | 34.5 |
| 1975 | 541 | 48.6 |
| 1976* | 603 | 50.6 |

*May

*Source: Hansard,* 19 April 1977, Vol.903, col.64.

and ministers' predictions, it appears that unemployment is likely to become a more common cause of poverty during the next few years. Just how significant a cause of family poverty can be seen from the table below which looks at the growth in the numbers of unemployed drawing supplementary benefits and expresses these totals for the different years as a percentage of all beneficiaries below pensionable age dependent on supplementary allowances. During 1977 unemployment had once again become the single most important reason why families were pushed into poverty.

*Action*

While it is immensely important to concentrate efforts on securing a return to full employment, it is also important to prevent those who are now bearing our unemployment from being poor, and two reforms are urgent. The National Insurance scheme must be made a more effective weapon against poverty. Beveridge envisaged unemployment benefit being payable so long as claimants were without jobs, providing they were registered for work. But together with extending the length of unemployment benefit we should consider paying it at a higher rate at least for those who remain unemployed for more than 12 months. Most claimants in this category are shown by both government research and that carried out by individuals to have been reduced to poverty. In addition the insurance scheme should face up to the fact of large scale youth unemployment. Many of them have never had the chance of working and so building up an adequate insurance record. Pupils during their last year at school should be credited with National Insurance contributions and so become eligible for unemployment benefit early on in their working lives – should God's gentle rain fall on them.

This reform needs to be enacted simultaneously with the development of a generous child benefit scheme. At the present time there is concern that a large proportion of the work force earns less than they could get in drawing benefit. There are 110,000 heads of households in full time work earning less than the state poverty line income. Paying the unemployed the higher National Insurance rate would mean a considerable improvement in the rate paid to the children of the unemployed. This must be matched by similar generous payments to the children of those in work. Such a move would not only raise the income of the very poorest – those who earn their poverty – but would also reinforce the incentive to take jobs when they become available. Child benefit is paid to the children of those in work, but deducted from the social security payments of those who are not part of the labour force. Therefore the more generous the child benefit payment, the larger the difference between income when in work and on benefit.

# 6 The Immigrant Community

**Samir Shah**

Samir Shah is researching at St. Catherines College, Oxford.

Immigrants have formed a small, but highly significant, part of the labour force of Western European industrialised economies since World War II. The Common Market countries, Austria, Norway, Sweden and Switzerland have all acted as receiving countries for immigrants from less developed ones — former colonies, Turkey, Yugoslavia, Spain, Greece and other Mediterranean countries, including parts of North Africa. Great Britain has primarily received migrants from her ex-colonies — West Indies, India, Pakistan, Bangladesh and East Africa. The main bulk of this immigration occurred during the late fifties and through the sixties. Migrant labour has played a key part in the growth-orientated policies of Western Europe. As Paine notes:

> "The end of the Korean War marked the start of two decades of unprecedented — if uneven — prosperity in advanced industrial economies, with rapid output growth rates overall being accompanied by historically low unemployment rates."[1]

Whilst the general expansion lasted, and the overall standard of living kept rising, the problems and deprivation suffered by the immigrant communities, in their new countries, were thought to be always capable of being solved. Problems were seen as linked to the nature of immigrant communities themselves and not to any wider 'class' problem. But the economic recession of the seventies and the consequent rise in unemployment, and its specific effect on immigrants, has forced analysis to investigate the effect of class on immigrant situations. In this chapter we propose to investigate these relations. The term "immigrant" by itself does not imply any specific class position.

As with any such empirical category, the meaning of the term may only be defined ostensively; its determination is specific to an actual situation at a particular period. The 1971 Census indicated that 69.5 per cent of those males born in the West Indies, India and Pakistan belonged to the manual working categories, compared with 50.6 per cent for all males. For females the figures were 39.3 per cent for these immigrants and 25.8 per cent for all females. For the professional classes, the figures are 9.7 per cent (immigrant male), 16.5 per cent (all males), and 3.3 per cent (immigrant female), 5.5 per cent (all female). A large part of the Indian birthplace group are known to be 'white' Indians of the higher social classes (up to 33 per cent); thus, even these figures are biased towards the professional classes. If we removed the Indian component, the working class nature of West Indians and Pakistanis is quite clear: 78 per cent of males and 41.6 per cent of females are manual workers, 4.6 per cent males and 1.3 per cent females are professionals. It is apparent that, although there are Asian doctors, Asian businessmen, West Indian nurses and so on, the vast majority of immigrants are working class. What we shall investigate here is the specific vulnerability of these working class immigrants to unemployment.[2]

The majority of immigrants are involved in jobs which are characterised more often than not, by several of these elements; (1) low pay, (2) unhealthy, unattractive working conditions, (3) low level of skill, a) arduous, b) manual, 4) anti-social hours, (5) piece-work pay systems, (6) fluctuations in work load/labour demand. In the last instance, it is the first of these elements – low pay – which determines one further, very important, correlative; the jobs are unattractive to, and are therefore unable to recruit, indigenous labour. (Whenever jobs are arduous, unattractive but relatively well-paid, e.g. mining, indigenous labour is found doing it.) The clothing industry is typical. It is deskilled and disaggregated so that many firms simply require operators on sewing machines; the industry itself is often to be found in Victorian back-to-back housing and tenements (e.g. London's East End), the working conditions, piece-work systems and seasonal fluctuations in work load scarcely make it attractive to young English girls who are able to opt for the more congenial atmosphere (and better pay) of offices and shops. The deskilling of jobs in certain other industries though mechanisation has also encouraged the employment of immigrants. Foundry works in metal manufacture now have jobs on direct production which require minimum training and which did not exist 10-15 years ago. In the West Midlands, 23.3 per cent of workers in iron castings were immigrants (1971). Textiles, in which mule spinning (3-4 years to learn) has been replaced by ring spinning (6 weeks to learn), is another high immigrant industry. Textiles also require shift working, and a very high proportion of night-shift is done by Asian men. Other jobs that require a good deal of night work also have high immigrant proportion, e.g. food manufacture, public transport, hotels and catering.

It is certainly the case that the specific working class position of the majority of immigrants has put them in the front line of all manner of disadvantages. This was noted by several commentaries on the sixties. Thus Wright says:

> "The general picture emerges that coloured unemployment rates are higher than white, and in all probability, as Wood suggests, at least twice as high if not higher."[3]

Rose, looking at the evidence for unemployment during the sixties wrote:

> "What is noteworthy about these movements is that when the level of unemployment rises the proportion of immigrants amongst the total unemployed also rises. Thus, in times of rising unemployment Commonwealth immigrants tend to be harder hit than the general population."[4]

This pattern is not peculiar to Great Britain. Castles and Kosack, referring to Lednet's study[5] in France say:

> "A detailed study on unemployment in France comes to the conclusion that national or ethnic minorities always tend to have higher unemployment rates than the majority groups."[6]

In their review of studies on unemployment amongst immigrant groups, and of their own work, Castles and Kosack conclude:

> ". . . it is, on the whole true to say that they [immigrant workers] suffer more from it [unemployment] than the indigenous populations."[7]

That is the evidence of the sixties. What of the seventies?

The pattern in Table 6.I should now come as no surprise. As unemployment has risen through the seventies, so the proportion of the unemployed that are from minority groups has risen. The present unemployment rate stands at 6.8 per cent (August 1977). The minority groups constitute 4 per cent of the total unemployed. Since up-to-date economic activity rates are not available for the minority groups, we cannot ascertain whether the proportion of immigrants who are unemployed from the total number of economically active immigrants is significantly different from the total unemployment rate. However, we can measure the rate of increase of unemployment amongst immigrant workers and the total population. Table 6.II illustrates the percentage increases in unemployment from November 1973 to August 1977. There was a 206.3 per cent increase in unemployment during this period for the population as a whole. For minority workers it was a 480.6 per cent increase. Breaking down these figures by sex, we can see that it is the female workforce that has been particularly badly hit: a remarkable 1000.7 per cent increase in unemployment for female minority group workers, with an increase of 505.2 per cent for the total female workforce.

Neither unemployment nor minority groups form homogenous entities. Unemployment varies according to region, age, sex and occupation. Immigrants themselves constitute widely differing groups which are, both individually and severally, distributed unevenly across the four categories of unemployment variance. To comprehend fully the present state of the relationship between immigrant workers and unemployment, we need to unravel the interrelationships between the different categories.

Tables 3.IV, 4.II and III, and 6.III-V, illustrate the state of unemployment according to the factors enumerated above. This much is clear: unemployment has hit most severely the 'extremities' of the UK (North, N.West, Wales, S.West, Scotland, N.Ireland) leaving the S.E. Midlands and Anglia at par, or just below, levels; the younger age-brackets, females and the occupations of the lower social classes have also suffered relatively more. Tables 6.VI-IX break down the immigrant communities according to these categories. We can see that immigrant workers are generally younger and occupy positions at the lower end of labour market. On the other hand, the proportion of female workers, particularly for the Asian communities, is lower and their regional distribution indicates concentration in the Midlands and the South-East.

It would appear, then, that two factors contribute towards high unemployment (occupation and age-structure), and two against (regional distribution and sex-structure). The reality is that immigrants have higher unemployment rates regardless of these factors. At the regional level, we can see from Table 6.IX that over the period November 1973 to August 1977, most of the Standard Regions contributed roughly the same proportion to the total of unemployed minority workers. The relative contributions of the North, Wales and Scotland decreased and consequently there was a below average percentage increase in unemployment. This was 'compensated' by a 595.6 per cent increase in E. Anglia and 573.3 per cent increase in the South-West. Nevertheless, the main areas of immigrant unemployment (Midlands and South-East) remained the same from 1973 to 1977. This is, of course, partly a simple reflection of the fact that the vast majority of immigrants live in the Midlands and the South-East. On the other hand, the largest relative increases in unemployment has been in the areas of high immigrant concentration, South-East (291 per cent) and West Midlands and East

**Table 6.I: Minority Group Unemployment**

| | *Total Minority Group Unemployed* | | | *Minority Group Unemployed as a % of Total Unemployed* | | | *Unemployment Rate G.B.* |
|---|---|---|---|---|---|---|---|
| | *Male* | *Female* | *Total* | *Male* | *Female* | *Total* | |
| Feb. 1974 | 11440 | 2106 | 13546 | 2.3 | 2.3 | 2.3 | 2.6 |
| Aug. 1974 | 12571 | 2764 | 15335 | 2.3 | 2.3 | 2.3 | 2.8 |
| Feb. 1975 | 17013 | 4309 | 21322 | 2.7 | 3.2 | 2.8 | 3.3 |
| Aug. 1975 | 32261 | 9926 | 42187 | 3.6 | 3.4 | 3.5 | 4.8 |
| Feb. 1976 | 35852 | 11090 | 46942 | 3.7 | 4.0 | 3.7 | 5.5 |
| Aug. 1976 | 42736 | 16334 | 59070 | 4.1 | 4.2 | 4.1 | 6.3 |
| Feb. 1977 | 36031 | 13766 | 49797 | 3.5 | 4.2 | 3.6 | 5.9 |
| Aug. 1977 | 44084 | 18349 | 62438 | 4.0 | 3.9 | 4.0 | 6.8 |

*Source: Dept. of Employment Gazette,* v.85, Unit of Manpower Studies, p.111, March 1977,p.256; June 1977, p.610; September 1977, p.964.

**Table 6.II: Growth of Minority Group Unemployment**

| | *Minority Group Unemployment* | | | *Total Persons G.B.* | | |
|---|---|---|---|---|---|---|
| | *Male* | *Female* | *Total* | *Male* | *Female* | *Total* |
| Nov. 1973 | 9087 | 1667 | 10754 | 416054 | 77507 | 493561 |
| Aug. 1977 | 44084 | 18349 | 62438 | 1097933 | 469080 | 1567013 |
| % Increases | 385.2 | 1000.7 | 480.6 | 163.9 | 505.2 | 206.3 |

*Source: DoE Gazette,* January 1974, v.82, p.66; *DoE Gazette,* September 1977, v.85, p.964.

**Table 6.III: Unemployment by Occupation, June 1977**

| | *Male* | *Female* | *Total* | *Notified Vacancies* |
|---|---|---|---|---|
| Managerial & Professional | 70053 | 25353 | 95406 | 15502 |
| Clerical and Related | 76662 | 97450 | 174142 | 25344 |
| Other non-Manual | 25969 | 40631 | 66600 | 14424 |
| Craft and other similar | 143324 | 8300 | 151624 | 42950 |
| General labourers | 368032 | 62554 | 430586 | 8124 |
| Other Manual | 227579 | 63546 | 291125 | 60460 |
| | | Total | 1209483 | Total 166804 |

*Source: DoE Gazette,* August 1977, v.85, p.821.

**Table 6.IV: Unemployment by Industry, June 1977**

| | *Aug. 1973* | *May 1974* | *May 1975* | *May 1976* | *May 1977* |
|---|---|---|---|---|---|
| Agriculture, Forestry, Fishing | 2.2 | 2.4 | 3.7 | 5.5 | 5.9 |
| Mining and quarrying | 4.7 | 4.4 | 4.2 | 4.7 | 4.5 |
| Manufacturing | 1.9 | 1.9 | 3.3 | 4.7 | 4.4 |
| Construction | 5.6 | 6.9 | 10.4 | 14.5 | 14.3 |
| Gas, Electricity and Water | 1.9 | 1.7 | 1.8 | 2.5 | 2.6 |
| Transport and Communications | 2.2 | 2.2 | 2.9 | 3.9 | 3.9 |
| Distribution | 1.8 | 1.8 | 2.9 | 4.5 | 4.7 |
| Financial, Professional & Misc. | 1.3 | 1.3 | 1.8 | 2.8 | 3.1 |
| Public Administration | 1.9 | 2.0 | 2.5 | 3.4 | 4.2 |

*Source: DoE Gazette,* July 1977, v.85, p.764.

**Table 6.V: Regional Distribution of Immigrants**

| *% Econ. Active* | *Born in New Commonwealth (Both parents born outside UK)* |
|---|---|
| South East | 59.6 |
| East Anglia | 0.8 |
| South West | 2.0 |
| West Midlands | 15.6 |
| East Midlands | 5.2 |
| Yorks & Humberside | 7.0 |
| North West | 7.0 |
| North | 0.9 |
| Wales | 0.8 |
| Scotland | 1.2 |

*Source: Unit for Manpower Studies,* 1977, p.112, based on Census 1971, Special Tabulation DT 1746, and Econ. Activity Table 2.

**Table 6.VI: Socio-Economic Distribution of Immigrants**

*Economically-Active Persons Born in*

| | *W. Indies* | | *Pakistan* | | *India* | | *E.Africa* | |
|---|---|---|---|---|---|---|---|---|
| | *male* | *female* | *male* | *female* | *male* | *female* | *male* | *female* |
| Employers, Managers and Professional | 2.8 | 0.8 | 7.5 | 9.1 | 17.2 | 7.1 | 17.3 | 4.1 |
| Intermediate and Junior Non-Manual and Personal Service | 8.2 | 45.8 | 8.3 | 46.9 | 16.8 | 47.6 | 24.0 | 51.7 |
| Formen and Supervisors – Manual | 1.0 | 0.2 | 0.6 | 0.2 | 1.5 | 0.2 | 1.0 | 0.3 |
| Skilled Manual | 39.5 | 7.3 | 20.8 | 6.1 | 25.6 | 6.4 | 24.7 | 9.8 |
| Semi-skilled Manual | 23.6 | 28.0 | 32.7 | 18.0 | 20.5 | 23.3 | 19.5 | 24.2 |
| Unskilled Manual | 15.8 | 7.4 | 22.8 | 2.2 | 11.1 | 5.2 | 4.4 | 1.6 |
| Farmers, Agric. workers Armed Forces, Self-employed | 2.6 | 0.6 | 3.0 | 2.9 | 4.6 | 2.1 | 5.3 | 1.2 |
| Indefinite | 6.5 | 10.0 | 4.2 | 14.7 | 2.7 | 8.1 | 3.8 | 7.3 |

*Source:* Unit for Manpower Studies, 1977, pp.145-6, based on Census 1971.

**Table 6.VII: Immigrant Age Structure**

| | *% total Minority Group** | *% of Total G.B.* |
|---|---|---|
| 0-14 | 40.8 | 23.9 |
| 15-24 | 17.0 | 14.6 |
| 25-44 | 31.9 | 24.1 |
| 45+ | 10.3 | 37.4 |

*Born in New Commonwealth with both parents born in New Commonwealth.
*Source: Census 1971,* Country of Birth Tables p.8 and p.12.

**Table 6.VIII: Sex Structure of Immigrant Groups**
*(Economically Active Persons)*

| | *Male* | *Female* | *Ratio m/f* |
|---|---|---|---|
| West Indies | 124820 | 90120 | 1.39 |
| Pakistan | 76930 | 5930 | 12.97 |
| India | 137840 | 51810 | 2.66 |
| East Africa | 20760 | 11570 | 1.79 |
| Great Britain | 15884000 | 9138000 | 1.74 |

*Source. Unit for Manpower Studies,* 1977, pp.145-146.

**Table 6.IX: Regional Unemployment Trends (Minority Group)**

| | *Nov. 1973* | *[col.%]* | *Aug.1977* | *[col.%]* | *% Increase* |
|---|---|---|---|---|---|
| South East | 4832 | [44.9] | 28853 | [46.2] | 497.1 |
| East Anglia | 68 | [ 0.6] | 473 | [ 0.8] | 595.6 |
| South West | 150 | [ 1.4] | 1010 | [ 1.6] | 573.3 |
| West Midlands | 2440 | [22.7] | 14979 | [24.0] | 513.9 |
| East Midlands | 1000 | [ 9.3] | 5615 | [ 9.0] | 461.5 |
| Yorks & Humb. | 783 | [ 7.3] | 4717 | [ 7.6] | 502.4 |
| North West | 1046 | [ 9.7] | 5583 | [ 8.9] | 433.7 |
| North | 118 | [ 1.1] | 458 | [ 0.7] | 288.1 |
| Wales | 77 | [ 0.7] | 263 | [ 0.4] | 241.5 |
| Scotland | 237 | [ 2.3] | 487 | [ 0.8] | 105.5 |
| Great Britain | 10754 | [100.0] | 62438 | [100.0] | 480.6 |

*Source: DoE Gazette,* January 1974, v.82, p.66; September 1977, v.85, p.964.

**Table 6.X: Unemployment Increases for Minority Group Workers**
*(Persons born in or whose parents were born in)*

| | *November '73** | | *Aug. 1977* | | *% Increase* | | *% Increase†* | |
|---|---|---|---|---|---|---|---|---|
| | *m* | *f* | *m* | *f* | *m* | *f* | *m* | *f* |
| Africa | 2230 | 295 | 8025 | 4467 | 259.8 | 1414.2 | 256.2 | 1304.7 |
| W. Indies | 2611 | 672 | 13719 | 6447 | 425.4 | 859.4 | 395.3 | 676.7 |
| India | 1612 | 343 | 9907 | 5285 | 514.6 | 1440.8 | 501.5 | 1323.4 |
| Pakistan and Bangladesh | 1413 | 81 | 8289 | 1373 | 486.6 | 1595.1 | 476.0 | 1195.3 |

*Excludes young persons
† % Increase with young persons included (young persons allocated 50:50, male, female)

*Source: DoE Gazette,* December 1974, v.82, p.66, September 1977, v.85, p.964.

**Table 6.XI: Unemployed Minority Group by Age**
*February 1977*

| | *16-17* | | *18-24* | | *25-39* | | *40+* | | |
|---|---|---|---|---|---|---|---|---|---|
| | *m* | *f* | *m* | *f* | *m* | *f* | *m* | *f* | *Total* |
| E.Africa | 205 | 180 | 1417 | 1158 | 1307 | 781 | 1847 | 396 | 7291 |
| W. Indies | 1329 | 993 | 3782 | 1676 | 3382 | 1030 | 3428 | 1093 | 16713 |
| India | 409 | 288 | 1747 | 1590 | 2146 | 1439 | 3046 | 906 | 11571 |
| Pakistan | 430 | 128 | 1685 | 377 | 1803 | 200 | 2271 | 83 | 6977 |
| Bangladesh | 48 | 9 | 143 | 18 | 375 | 319 | 690 | 20 | 1322 |

| | *% Unemployed 24 and under* |
|---|---|
| East Africa | 40.6 |
| W. Indies | 46.6 |
| India | 34.9 |
| Pakistan | 37.6 |
| Bangladesh | 16.5 |

*Source: DoE Gazette,* June 1977, v.85, p.611.

Midlands (300.1 per cent and 269 per cent respectively). Thus although the highest unemployment rates are to be found in areas of low immigrant settlement, recent trends have indicated that unemployment is rising faster in areas with high immigrant numbers.

The other factor which should have contributed against high unemployment rates for immigrants is their sex ratio. Although the absolute figures may be low, the percentage increases in immigrant female unemployment are so dramatic as to vitiate any compensating effect. It is also worth bearing in mind the high activity rates of immigrant women which also counteracts the effect of a high male-female ratio. Table 6.X illustrates these rises. Remembering that the average unemployment increase was 206.3 per cent (for females 505.2 per cent), the percentage increases of 676.7 per cent (West Indian females) to 1323.4 per cent (Indian females) are astounding.

We have already shown that unemployment particularly affects semi-skilled and unskilled labour (Table 6.III), and that immigrants are particularly employed in those categories (Table 6.VI). We have shown, too, a similar relationship exists in terms of youth unemployment (Table 6.VII). Table 6.XI breaks the figures by country of origin for February 1977. Note particularly that 46.6 per cent of West Indian unemployed are 24 or under.

We may conclude that all the factors by which unemployment varies throughout Great Britain act in some way to the detriment of the immigrant communities.

However, this extensive statistical analysis of the nature of immigrant unemployment provides us simply with the bare facts of the situation. To go further, we need to try and account for the specific vulnerability of immigrant workers to unemployment generally and during periods of economic recessions in particular. We may approach explanation at various levels depending on what criteria we use to demarcate causality. In this chapter we propose to investigate and evaluate a particular form of analysis which identifies a set of 'factors' which may be considered to have a significant effect on the nature of the relationship between immigrants and unemployment.

*Factoral Explanation*

This is arguably the most common form of explanation used not only on the present subject of study but generally on 'problems' of social science. The underlying method of this 'problem-solving' approach is to identify through empirical analysis, certain causal variables which bear a determining relationship to aspects of the 'problem': in this case, immigrant unemployment. A reading of several studies[8] on the subject under discussion reveals these 'types' of factors: (1) characteristics of the 'host' population, (2) characteristics of the immigrant population, (3) situational characteristics.

Type 1 factors include racial discrimination in forms of Recruitment, Access to training, Promotion and Redundancy.

Type 2 factors include Racial disadvantage, Low skills, Occupational structure, Age-structure, Unionisation.

Type 3 factors include Spatial location and Contingents of employment.

Of course, these factors do not act separately or in isolation. They combine in different ways in specific situations; the general effect of which is to increase immigrant susceptibility to unemployment.

*Type 1*

David Smith's recent synthesis of the PEP report on racial disadvantage concentrates on this aspect. Using extensive tests in which jobs were applied for by both white and black people, Smith concludes:

> "The results of the actor tests show that there are still substantial levels of discrimination against Asians and West Indians when applying for manual jobs; that the discrimination is stronger against applicants for non-skilled than for skilled jobs; that it is based on colour prejudice rather than prejudice against foreigners; and that levels of discrimination against Indians, Pakistanis and West Indians are much the same."[9]

One particular instance is worth recalling. A Pakistani boy aged 19 who spoke fluent English and had three A levels, said about an interview with the personnel manager of a large engineering firm "He told me that he has already got two apprentices of my race and these are enough".[10] Other aspects of discrimination are also important. Smith notes a reluctance for employers to promote Asians and West Indians to supervisory positions (for fear of white resentment) and discriminatory practices with respect to training opportunities.[11] The Unit for Manpower Studies noting the under-representation of blacks at the supervisory level, and following an account of employers explanations (low turnover among existing supervisors, promotion system based on superiority), suggests

> "It is, of course, difficult to assess how far such explanations for there being relatively few black supervisors are merely a rationalisation for discriminating practices."[12] p.73-74.

This form of discrimination is also noted elsewhere.[13] Discrimination in terms of redundancy is also prevalent. Thus, a study of a small factory provided a case of discriminatory policies, based on a general lack of knowledge amongst the employers of the criteria for redundancy. Smith says

> "Before automation 80 men were employed in this department, of whom 40 were West Indians. At the time of our visit the department employed 35, of whom six were West Indians. Thus about 10 out of 40 whites were made redundant, compared with 34 out of 40 West Indians."[14]

We may conclude on Type 1 factors as demonstrating the simple fact that racist attitudes amongst employers not only keep blacks in a disadvantaged position in the occupational structure so that they are susceptible to unemployment when employed, but actually getting employed itself becomes difficult.

*Type 2*

This category of factors provides the most common set of reasons for the explanation of immigrant problems. They locate the difficulties firmly within the communities themselves.

Racial disadvantage involves such factors as the low-level of English-speaking ability to be found amongst immigrant groups – particularly the Asian communities. This, in turn, makes them less employable and restricts the range of employment available to them. The UMS note that

> "In those areas where Asians account for a high proportion of New Commonwealth immigrants, their much greater cultural, and language differences from the indigenous population than those of, for example, West Indians, adds to the difficulties involved in integrating workers from racial minorities with the labour force and in removing barriers to equal opportunity."[15]

This racial disadvantage has, of course, further correlations. Conditions of employment, contracts, rights and obligations all get submerged with the lack of simple communication. Employees with few rights or no knowledge of rights are, of course, much easier to dismiss during periods of recession. Other characteristics of immigrant workers are also seen as contributing to their vulnerability. Thus, the well-known immigrant desire to earn money above all else, explains their 'willingness' to work on shifts, to work long hours under poor conditions and so on. The UMS comment on the labour force of the London Brick Company's works is typical:

> "The firm has successively recruited substantial numbers of Poles, European Volunteer Workers, Italians, West Indians and finally Indians and Pakistanis. The high proportion of immigrants in their labour force is attributable to there being insufficient indigenous workers willing to do the heavy and unattractive, though well-paid, jobs they have to offer. Most jobs are relatively simple, requiring little intelligence, but physically arduous and often involve working in hot and dusty conditions on alternate day and night shifts."[16]

Other factors such as the low-level of skills, poor educational qualifications are also causal in their implications, particularly for the young immigrants. Fyfe has discussed the impact of youth unemployment generally, and we have shown that the young people are in a particularly poor position.[17] Young Blacks are seen as doubly disadvantaged, thus Smith says

> "The educational level of a section of Asian and West Indian youth is probably particularly low, because they have had difficulty in adapting to the British educational system, and the system has done little to adapt itself to them. This, combined with racial discrimination, may be the reason for high level of unemployment among young people from the minority groups."[18]

But low skills, poor qualifications and the consequent weak position in the labour market are not confined to immigrant youth. It is a fact of existence of many immigrant workers. As the above statistical analysis has shown, this fact situates the majority of immigrant workers in certain sectors of the occupational structure; and it is these sectors that are adversely affected during recessions. What is disturbing is that immigrant youth are also, through their lack of skills, occupying the same poor positions: thus the propensity for unemployment to affect blacks in particular becomes trans-generational.

Another factor which weakens immigrant workers is in situations of non-unionisation. Contrary to expectations, minority group workers are very quick to join unions and their membership rates are higher than the white population, particularly for male workers. It is, however, somewhat less for minority group women, and particularly low for Moslem working women. It is one thing, though, to be a union member and another to find that this membership helps in the security of jobs. Smith notes the employment of Indians as 'casuals' in a London bakery despite working continuously over long periods:

> "The managing director explained the advantages of the system in these terms: they are on an hour's notice and there is no chance of redundancies and industrial trouble."[19]

But

> "The union membership in that bakery had been built up entirely by Indians who maintained that the casual labour situation would not be tolerated by white workers. The union's full-time official had taken no action . . . this is the kind of situation that the union would be expected to deal with if the workers were white; certainly they had made no special efforts . . . "

Casual labour has historically been a role played by immigrant workers. Stedman-Jones' study of casual labour in Victorian London discusses the practice of such workers in the clothing industry.[21] The author's own study of the industry in the East End illustrated the extremely weak position of immigrant women employed in those parts of the production process requiring few skills. Membership of unions was practically non-existent and the women were extremely susceptible to the seasonality of production inherent in the fashion trade. But more than this: the lack of any formal organisational strength weakened their bargaining position absolutely, and, of course, during any severe cut-back in the trade, they were the most likely to suffer unemployment, and with no form of compensation.[22]

Type 2 factors are pathological. Certain characteristics of the immigrant communities are seen as conducive to keeping them in a weak and vulnerable position. If the problem lies within the immigrant communities, the solution lies with them as well.

*Type 3*

The first factor within this type is related to the spatial distribution of immigrant communities at both the regional level, and the city-level. The UMS state quite categorically that one of the reasons for unemployment amongst racial minority groups is the:

> ". . . greater percentage increases in unemployment in regions – for example, the South-East and W. Midlands – which racial minority groups are concentrated than in Great Britain as a whole."[23]

Our own analysis earlier also noted the higher increases in unemployment in areas of high immigrant concentrations. Whereas immigrants first came to regions of low unemployment, economic recession is seen to have 'caught up' with them. These regions (South East, Midlands) are now experiencing increasing unemployment, and immigrants, by virtue of their spatial location, are inevitably experiencing a rise in unemployment rate.

The second aspect of the spatial solution is intra-city distribution. The segregation of immigrant communities and their concentration in inner-city areas is well-known and well-documented.[24] It is also a fact that there has been considerable movement of industry away from city-centre locations to peripheral sites. Together with the decay of urban fabric (housing conditions, amenities, schools, etc.) a syndrome known as 'multiple deprivation' exists in inner-city areas, particularly in areas of immigrant concentration. Thus within the city, employment opportunities are scarce in these areas. Immigrants live in these areas: therefore, immigrants are prone to unemployment. Every major city in Great Britain has its examples: Eversley and Donnison have documented it for London; CDP reports on the Poverty Programme illustrate the problems as do the Inner Area studies on Liverpool, Birmingham and London; Demuth has reviewed the various government initiatives on such urban deprivation.[25] The final factor in Type 3 is related to the theory that minority groups function as a marginal source of labour. This theory suggests that minority unemployment rate fluctuates with the general level of unemployment with respect of short-term changes. Thus during the sixties there was a pattern of short-term changes in unemployment, which was correlated with equally short-term changes of minority unemployment rates.[26] The UMS link this with the shorter average duration in employment of minority group workers and are thus vulnerable to the "last in, first out" rules at times of redundancy.[27] We can see this factor operating on occupations with marked seasonal fluctuations of employment (construction, clothing) as well as those which are very susceptible to changes in the purchasing power of consumers (fashion trades, service and catering industries).

Type 3 factors, then, are external both to the immigrant population and to the host population. They lie in the realms of marginal economics and in the historical development of both Great Britain and individual cities. Immigrant communities have found themselves within this uneven spatial matrix and may be seen to be adversely affected by the resultant conditions of existence.

This concludes our account of factors explaining the relationship between immigrants and unemployment. The list may not have been exhaustive but we hope we have covered the major determinants. There are, however, several theoretical and conceptual problems associated with this type of enumeration.[28] This is not to say that these factors do not operate, indeed, the reality of their operation is evidenced by the figures of immigrant unemployment. Racist attitudes, racial disadvantage and deprived spatial situations are real enough: the question is whether these factors, which exist and operate individually and in combination, are merely conjunctural phenomenon. In other words, can we, after this process of classification and categorisation, assert a causal status on these factors and consequently exclude the factors themselves from analysis? If this is the case, we are assuming that the structure of the whole does not have any effect on the behaviour of aspects of the whole.

Policy recommendations based on this kind of factoral study have precisely this assumption: problems (and therefore solutions) operate within a neutral consensual system in which different parts may be isolated and examined relatively independent of each other. This position is clearly untenable if we view society as containing structural contradictions. These structural contradictions effect and influence the state of affairs that exist within society and behaviour within that state of affairs.

In this particular case, we are concerned with the attempts of capital to re-establish the rate of surplus value through the use of a specific type of labour (i.e. immigrant workers) in certain sectors of the economy (semi-skilled and unskilled manual labour).[29] The rate of surplus value is enhanced through lowering costs of production (low pay; poor conditions of work; intensification of production – shift work, long hours, piece-work based pay systems; inadequate security and weak legal positions thereby cutting costs in terms of redundancy, sickness, holiday insurance, pensions etc.) and costs of social reproduction (costs involved in the housing, feeding, clothing of the worker and the worker's family; also costs involved in collective facilities: amenities, schools, welfare services).[30]

The whole object of the massive use of migrant labour was to enable this reduction of costs of production and reproduction. The peculiar vulnerability of immigrant labour stems from their specific role in the economy and from their marginal position to the indigenous labour movement (which is why their costs of production and reproduction are lower than average[31]). The weak power relations of the class fraction immigrant labour are a result of the factors mentioned above; and, importantly, are a necessary aspect of the post-war development of the British social formation.[32]

The various factors which have been enumerated can no longer be seen as a result of unfortunate circumstances: they are the concrete effects of the ensemble of structures that define the present social system. Structural analyses in other parts of this book, and elsewhere,[33] have shown that it is tendency and counter-tendency within the capitalist mode of production,[34] and the nature and state of class relations, that are the real determinants of what we 'see' around us – including racial discrimination, racial disadvantage and all the specificities of the vulnerability of immigrant labour. Factors certainly do exist: they are the concrete workings of the processes which determine the specific characteristics of the subject under discussion. To go further than this requires a thorough investigation of the structures and controlling mechanisms that not only determine the concrete forms of such factors, but also shows that their very existence is the observable 'effects' of a 'combination of elements'[35] specific to the nature of Western European advanced economies.

**FOOTNOTES**

1. Paine, S.H. 'The Changing Role of Migrant Workers in the Advanced Capitalist Economies of Western Europe' in Griffiths, R.T. (ed.) *Government Business and Labour in European Capitalism,* 1977.
2. Although immigrants to Great Britain have included several 'white' groups – Irish, Greek Cypriots, Maltese, etc. – the term as used in this chapter (as with the other related terms 'minority group' and 'New Commonwealth') will refer generally to the 'coloured' immigrant.
3. Wright, P. *The Coloured Worker in British Industry,* 1968, p.55. OUP.
4. Rose, E.J.B., et.al., *Colour and Citizenship,* 1969, p.150. OUP.
5. Lednet, R., *Sociologie du Chômage,* 1966, Presses Universitaires de France.
6. Castles, S., and Kosack, G., *Immigrant Workers and Class Structure in Western Europe,* 1973, p.87. OUP.
7. Ibid., p.92.
8. Allen, S., *New Minorities, Old Conflicts,* 1971, Random House; Banton, M., *Racial Minorities,* 1972, Fontana; Castles, S. and Kosack G., *op.cit.;* Daniel, W.W., *Racial Discrimination in England,* 1971, Pelican; Hiro, D., *Black British, White British,* 1973, Pelican; Patterson, S., *Immigrants in Industry,* 1968, OUP; Patterson, S., *Immigration and Race Relations in Britain, 1960-1970,* 1969,

OUP; Peach, G.C.K., *West Indian Migration to Britain,* 1968, OUP; Richmond, A., *Migration and Race Relations in our English City,* 1973, OUP; Smith, D., *Racial Disadvantage in Britain,* 1977, Pelican; Unit for Manpower Studies, *The Role of Immigrants in the Labour Market,* 1977, DoE; Wright, P., *op.cit.*

9. Smith, D., *op.cit.,* p.111.
10. Ibid., p.136.
11. Ibid., p.190.
12. Unit for Manpower Studies, *op.cit.,* pp.73-74.
13. Wright, P., *op.cit.,* p.76; Daniel, *op.cit.,* p.108; Castles and Kosack, *op.cit.,* p.109.
14. Smith, D., *op.cit.,* p.147.
15. Unit for Manpower Studies, *op.cit.,* p.29.
16. Ibid., p.38.
17. Fyfe, J., "Youth Unemployment: International Experience" in Griffiths, R.T., *op.cit.*
18. Smith, D., *op.cit.,* p.327.
19. Ibid., p.143.
20. Ibid, p.200.
21. Stedman-Jones, G., *Outcast London,* 1976, Peregrine.
22. Shah, S., "Immigrants and Employment in the Clothing Industry, the Rag Trade in London's East End", 1975, Runnymede Trust.
23. Unit for Manpower Studies, *op.cit.,* p.28.
24. See, for example, Timms, D.W.G., *The Urban Mosaic,* 1971, CUP; Peach, G.C.K. (ed.) *Urban Social Segregation,* 1975, Longmans; Bermant C., *Point of Arrival,* 1975, Eyre and Methun; Garrard, J.A., *The English and Immigration,* 1971, OUP; Lee, T.R., *Race and Residence – the Concentration and Dispersal of Immigrants in London,* 1977, OUP.
25. Donnison, D. and Everseley, D. (eds) *London: Urban Patterns, Problems and Policies,* 1973, Heinemann; CDP, "Gilding the Ghetto", 1977, Home Office; CDP "Coventry and Hillfields: Prosperity and the Persistence of Inequality", Part I, Final Report, 1975, Home Office; Demuth, C., "Government Initiatives on Urban Deprivation", 1977, Runnymede Trust Briefing Paper.
26. Smith, D., *op.cit.,* p.69.
27. Unit for Manpower Studies, *op.cit.,* p.28.
28. For a thorough critique of this 'common-sensical' approach see, Shah, S., "Some Aspects of the Geographic Analysis of Immigrants in London", D.Phil thesis (in prep.) Oxford University, see also, Allen, V.L. *Social Analysis,* 1975, pp. 69-88, Longmans.
29. For an economic analysis of this ' thirst for surplus value' see Mandel, E., *Marxist Economic Theory,* 1968, Merlin; Sweezy, P.M., *The Theory of Capitalist Development,* 1970, Monthly Review Press; Baran, P.A. and Sweezy, P.M. *Monopoly Capital,* 1966, pp.249-280. Monthly Review Press. For more specific analysis, see Castells, M. "Immigrant Workers and Class Struggles in Advanced Capitalism: the Western European Experience", *Politics and Society,* 1975, pp.33-66; Jones, K. and Smith A.D., *The Economic Impact of Commonwealth Immigration,* 1970, CUP; Berger, J. and Mohr, J., *A Seventh Man,* 1975, Pelican; Peach, G.C.K., 1968, *op.cit.*; Paine, S.H. *Exporting Workers: The Turkish Case,* 1974, CUP; Paine, S.H. 1977, *op.cit.*
30. C. Castells, M., 1975, *op.cit.;* Castells, M., *The Urban Question,* 1977, Edward Arnold; Pickvance, C.G. (ed.) *Urban Sociology* particularly the articles by Castells, Lamarche, Lojkine, 1976, Tavistock.

31. By the average we mean the standard of acceptable living and working conditions achieved by the labour movement in the history of a particular society.
32. Balibar, E., defines a 'social formation' as "the concrete complex whole comprising economic practice and ideological practice at a certain place and stage of development" in Althusser, L. and Balibar, E., *Reading Capital*, 1975, NLB, p.313.
33. See, particularly, Castells, M., 1975, *op.cit.;* Berger and Mohr, *op.cit.*
34. For an analysis of these tendencies and counter-tendencies, see Mandel, E., *op.cit.*, pp.132-81.
35. For a discussion of this type of metonymic causation, and the specific meaning of the terms 'effect' and 'combination of element', see Althusser and Balibar *op.cit.*, pp.13-69.

# PART THREE

## How the Government Reversed Labour Policies and the Post-War Consensus

# 7 The Stages of Sin . . .

**Brian Sedgemore**

Luton West MP, Brian Sedgemore is PPS to Tony Benn.

*The Problem*

On September 26 1974 speaking at Beech Hill School in Luton, the Chancellor of the Exchequer, Denis Healey, described the policy of controlling inflation through unemployment as "sin". In October of that same year the Labour Party committed itself in its manifesto to "restore and sustain full employment". At that time (October 1974) 648,000 people were out of work in the UK or 2.7% of the working population. In January of 1977 1,448,200 people were out of work or 6.1% of the working population. In May, the last count at the time that this paper was written, 1,341,700 were unemployed in the UK (5.7%).

In the medium term, i.e. over the next 2 years, in the run-up to the election the situation is hardly likely to improve much unless policies are changed. Indeed it could get worse. There are three reasons for this. The first and most important reason lies in the low growth policies of the Treasury, despite the medium-term financial soundness of an economy with North Sea Oil coming on stream on time. The last Public Expenditure White Paper (Command 6721-1) envisages economic growth of 2-3% per annum for the coming years whilst the last budget envisaged economic growth of only 1½% for the current financial year. These figures have to be set against the need of the economy to grow by some 3% per annum in normal circumstances merely to stop unemployment rising. The second reason lies in the stated government policy of holding public sector employment at its present levels between now and 1980. The third lies in the number of newcomers coming on to the market. According to the Department of Employment Gazette (December 1975) we can expect a growth in the total size of the labour market of 774,000 (excluding students) in the period 1976-1981.

The Chancellor has in effect adopted a policy of tackling inflation through unemployment and ended up with high unemployment and high rates of inflation, the latter being significantly fuelled until recently by the Treasury's exchange rate devaluation policy. Full employment is no longer an object of economic policy for the Treasury. They argue, privately, that it is not within the power of the government, any government, to secure a return to full employment and it would be wrong to attempt to do so. On their strategy full employment if ever it is to return can only do so as an accident of free trade miraculously thrown up by the policies of the USA and Germany.

One of the major problems which the Labour movement has to face up to is that although the central economic strategy has been opposed in a number of places (e.g. by individual trade unions, by the Cambridge Economic Policy Group, by the Tribune Group of MPs) the TUC itself, whose real power is greater than that of all those groups put together, has only paid lip-service to the idea of a coherent alternative economic strategy. Presumably they would disagree with the Cambridge Economic Policy Group (March 1977) in their assessment that "if unemployment had been held down to, say, three quarters of a million, the total real national income would be nearly 10% higher than it is, public expenditure cuts would have been unnecessary, industrial capacity and investment would be much higher than they are now". Unless the TUC twists the government's arm more over its central economic strategy I can see little hope of tackling the problems of unemployment other than at the periphery.

*Regional unemployment*

**Table 7.I: Areas worst hit by unemployment. Percentage unemployed 14th April 1977 over 10%**

| *Local areas (by region)* | | *Counties (by region)* | |
|---|---|---|---|
| *Strabane | 26.6 | Western Isles | 15.7 |
| Irvine | 12.2 | Cornwall | 11.3 |
| Wrexham | 11.5 | Merseyside Metropolitan | 10.5 |
| Wearside | 11.2 | Clwyd | 10.5 |
| Bargoed | 11.1 | Gwynedd | 10.5 |
| Liverpool | 10.8 | | |
| North Lanarkshire | 10.6 | | |
| Torbay | 10.5 | | |

*Nearly every local area in Northern Ireland has more than 10 per cent unemployment and Strabane, the worst area, is the only area cited.

*Source: Department of Employment*

**Table 7.II: Comparative Unemployment 1951-76 Annual Averages**

| | *U.K.* | | *Sweden* | *Germany* |
|---|---|---|---|---|
| | *Nos.* | % | % | % |
| 1951 | 281,400 | 1.3 | 1.8 | 9.0 |
| 1952 | 462,500 | 2.2 | 2.3 | 8.4 |
| 1953 | 380,000 | 1.8 | 2.8 | 7.5 |
| 1954 | 317,800 | 1.5 | 2.6 | 7.0 |
| 1955 | 264,500 | 1.2 | 2.5 | 5.1 |
| 1956 | 287,100 | 1.3 | 1.7 | 4.0 |
| 1957 | 347,200 | 1.6 | 1.9 | 3.4 |
| 1958 | 500,900 | 2.2 | 2.5 | 3.5 |
| 1959 | 512,100 | 2.3 | 2.0 | 2.4 |
| 1960 | 392,800 | 1.7 | 1.4 | 1.2 |
| 1961 | 376,800 | 1.6 | 1.2 | 0.8 |
| 1962 | 499,900 | 2.1 | 1.3 | 0.7 |
| 1963 | 612,300 | 2.6 | 1.4 | 0.8 |
| 1964 | 413,400 | 1.7 | 1.1 | 0.7 |
| 1965 | 359,700 | 1.5 | 1.1 | 0.6 |
| 1966 | 390,900 | 1.6 | 1.4 | 0.7 |
| 1967 | 599,100 | 2.5 | 1.7 | 2.1 |
| 1968 | 586,000 | 2.5 | 2.0 | 1.5 |
| 1969 | 580,900 | 2.5 | 1.7 | 0.8 |
| 1970 | 618,000 | 2.6 | 1.4 | 0.7 |
| 1971 | 799,100 | 3.5 | 2.0 | 0.8 |
| 1972 | 885,500 | 3.9 | 2.0 | 1.1 |
| 1973 | 630,200 | 2.7 | 1.9 | 1.2 |
| 1974 | 631,000 | 2.6 | 1.5 | 2.6 |
| 1975 | 997,600 | 4.2 | 1.4 | 4.7 |
| 1976 | 1,358,800 | 5.8 | 1.2 | 4.6 |
| 1977 (3 months only) | | 6.0 | | 5.2 |

*Note on table:* National figures are collated on different bases and care must be used in making comparisons. The U.K. figures are registered unemployed. The German figures come from registered unemployment exchange statistics. The Swedish figures relate to members of unemployment insurance funds.

Table 3.IV shows that there are still considerable disparities in employment between regions despite post-war regional policies.

But even these disparities do not reflect the true picture or show up the terrible problems that exist within regions. Table 7.I attempts to do this showing those towns and counties with the highest levels of unemployment.

These figures compare with the lowest unemployment levels of 1.6% for Hertford and 3% for Hertfordshire in the South East. They call for a review of the working of regional policies and a closer look to see how planning agreements and the National Enterprise Board can help.

*Post-War theory and experience*

The concept of full employment as an objective of economic policy was formulated by Keynes but did not become politically respectable until the war-time Beveridge Reports. In *Full Employment in a Free Society* (1944) Beveridge said this of full employment:

> "It means having always more vacant jobs than unemployed men. It means that the jobs are at fair wages, of such a kind and so located that the unemployed men can reasonably be expected to take them; it means, by consequence, that the normal lag between losing one job and finding another will be very short."

In the light of post-war experience and in the expectancy of postwar dislocation Beveridge put the acceptable level of unemployment at 3% of the working population, clearly implying that once post-war dislocation was over a lower figure might be more realistic. Hugh Gaitskell subsequently produced a similar norm. A more up to date definition was given by John Fraser MP in an answer to a Parliamentary question on 21 November 1974 when he said "Full employment is best defined as a situation in which an unemployed person can obtain a suitable job without undue delay. It does not admit of precise definition in quantitative terms" but a few days later (2 December 1974) another Department of Employment Minister did say in the Commons that the then present level of unemployment was unacceptable.

In fact as Table 7.II shows between 1951 and 1966 the highest annual average rate was 2.6% and in only four other years was the average annual rate 2% or more.

The position changed in the mid sixties when the number of unemployed increased considerably in relation to the number of job vacancies which was used as a measure of excess demand. It was thought, without much evidence, that this was partly due to the introduction of redundancy payments and earnings-related benefits.

Two theories gained currency at the time. One suggested that a certain level of unemployment (2-2½% was suggested as an appropriate figure for the time) was desirable to keep wage demands within bounds. Variations on this theme will no doubt recur when free collective bargaining is restored but with unemployment figures two to three times as high being suggested as appropriate for our time.

The other theory was that of the "shake-out". As Harold Wilson put it on 20 July 1966 (Hansard Col.628) "What is needed is a shake-out which will release the nation's manpower, skilled and semi-skilled and lead to a more purposive use of labour for the sake of increasing

**Table 7.III: Loss of Jobs in Manufacturing Industry, 1966-1976 (Great Britain)**

*(in thousands)*

| | *Nos Employed* | *Loss* |
|---|---|---|
| 1966 | 8,408 | –256 |
| 1967 | 8,152 | –256 |
| 1968 | 8,072 | – 80 |
| 1969 | 8,181 | +109 |
| 1970 | 8,164 | – 17 |
| 1971 | 7,886 | –278 |
| 1972 | 7,613 | –273 |
| 1973 | 7,664 | + 51 |
| 1974 | 7,705 | + 41 |
| 1975 | 7,334 | –371 |
| 1976 | 7,136 | –198 |
| Loss between 1966 and 1976: | 1,272 | |

*Sources:* March 1975 Dept. of Employment Gazette for 1966-1973, pp.196-7,
May 1977 Dept. of Employment Gazette for 1974-76.

exports and give effect to other national priorities." Lord Kahn, the Emeritus Professor of Economics at the University of Cambridge, in the Lloyds Bank Review wrote a decade later (January 1976) "It is important that when at long last our exports do recover with a recovery of world trade, such a recovery (and equally the increases in the production of import substitutes) should not at some stage be held back by physical shortages of labour. A reserve army of unemployed is needed to enable investment to recover . . . and at the appropriate moment in time, to enable personal consumption not only to recover but to rise at a modest pace."

The argument has a certain superficial attraction. It is all too true that we need to widen our manufacturing base and create more jobs in manufacturing industry and it is true that while the number of jobs in the public sector (and in the private service sector) has been rising over the past decade, the number in manufacturing industry has been falling (see Tables 7.III and IV).

But what is also true is that at the same time the level of unemployment – the "reserve army" as Lord Kahn euphemistically calls it – is growing not merely at the bottom of the trough in times of recession but at the peak of the boom in upturns. This too is clear from the UK figures in Table 3. At the height of the boom in 1973 and compared with the

**Table 7.IV:**
**Employees in Production and Services, June 1966-1976**
*Numbers and as a percentage of employees in employment*
*(in thousands)*

| | *Production (a)* | | *Employees in* | *Services (b)* | |
|---|---|---|---|---|---|
| | *No.* | *%* | *employment* | *No.* | *%* |
| 1966 | 11,567 | 50.8 | 22,787 | 11,220 | 49.2 |
| 1967 | 11,159 | 49.9 | 22,347 | 11,188 | 50.1 |
| 1968 | 10,943 | 49.3 | 22,186 | 11,243 | 50.7 |
| 1969 | 10,906 | 49.2 | 22,148 | 11,242 | 50.8 |
| 1970 | 10,701 | 48.7 | 21,993 | 11,292 | 51.3 |
| 1971 | 10,291 | 47.5 | 21,648 | 11,357 | 52.5 |
| 1972 | 10,012 | 46.2 | 21,650 | 11,638 | 53.8 |
| 1973 | 10,119 | 45.6 | 22,182 | 12,063 | 54.4 |
| 1974 | 10,083 | 45.2 | 22,297 | 12,214 | 54.8 |
| 1975 | 9,688 | 43.6 | 22,213 | 12,525 | 56.4 |
| 1976 | 9,423 | 42.8 | 21,997 | 12,574 | 57.2 |

(a) Including agriculture
(b) Services excluding private domestic service

*Source:* March 1975 Dept. of Employment Gazette for 1963-73, pp.196-7.
May 1977 Dept. of Employment Gazette for 1974-76.

previous peak in 1969, 90 per cent of manufacturing industry showed a fall in employment. But that was not because a "reserve" army of unemployed did not exist then. It did. Unemployment was still high (630,000) and manufacturing output was 7 per cent below that required to secure full employment and a strong balance of payments. It is difficult to know when the peak of the next boom will come but it is virtually certain that unemployment will be twice as high as was the peak of the 1973 boom and probably higher still. And then there is a downturn to follow.

It is absolutely clear from post-war experience that the growth of the public sector has played an important role in helping to sustain high levels of employment. Deprive it of that growth as the government is doing and there is no way of returning to full employment in the foreseeable future.

And yet somehow, somewhere along the line the government has taken hold of an alien argument to the effect that it is the growth of employment in the public sector which has been responsible for our failing industrial performance. A careful study of the evidence does not support that view. There is some evidence (compare Table 7.II with Tables 7.V and VI) that the growth of public sector employment in Sweden has helped to sustain full employment in the post-war years whilst not damaging its economic performance.

**Table 7.V: Public Employees in the U.K. and Sweden, 1965-75**

*(in thousands)*

| | | *1965* No. | *1965* % of total employed working population | *1975* No. | *1975* % of total employed working population |
|---|---|---|---|---|---|
| Employed working population | UK | 25,200 | 100.0 | 24,968 | 100.0 |
| | Sweden | 3,670 | 100.0 | 4,062 | 100.0 |
| Public sector total | UK | 5,970 | 23.7 | 7,278 | 29.1 |
| | Sweden | 670 | 18.2 | 1,244 | 30.6 |
| Central Government | UK | 1,800 | 7.1 | 2,246 | 9.0 |
| | Sweden | 240 | 6.5 | 341 | 8.4 |
| Public Corporations | UK | 2,020 | 8.0 | 2,008 | 8.0 |
| | Sweden | 200 | 5.4 | 250 | 6.2 |
| Local Authorities | UK | 2,150 | 8.5 | 3,024 | 12.1 |
| | Sweden | 230 | 6.5 | 653 | 16.1 |

*Sources.* National Income and Expenditure 1965-75, p.13.
Swedish Statistical Yearbook 1976, pp.238, 364-5, 241-2.

**Table 7.VI:**
**Economic Performance of U.K. and Sweden, 1965-75**

| | *Annual average percentage increase in GDP at purchasers values 1965-75* | *GDP per head (a)* *1965* £ | *GDP per head (a)* *1975* £ |
|---|---|---|---|
| U.K. | 2.2 | 840 | 999 |
| Sweden | 3.2 | 1,480 | 1,878 |

Note (a) 1970 prices and 1970 exchange rate

*Sources:* OECD National Accounts 1975, volume 1, pp.119 and 107.
Financial Statistics, May 1977, page 129.

*International Comparisons*

The note that accompanies Table 7.II has referred to the pitfalls in comparing unemployment figures produced on different bases for different countries. On a UK basis the German rate of unemployment should be reduced somewhat for a proper comparison. The July 1976 issue of the Department of Employment Gazette shows comparisons of figures for

Germany and Great Britain (*not* the United Kingdom) adjusted to the concepts used in the United States where the unemployment figures are based on a sample poll in various areas in which interviewers question a number of households on who is and is not seeking employment at the time of the interview. This method it is believed makes the United States' unemployment figures automatically higher than the UK figures.

**Table 7.VII:**
**International unemployment figures**
*(percentages)*

| | *Germany* | | *Great Britain* | |
|---|---|---|---|---|
| | *Unadjusted* | *Adjusted to U.S. concepts* | *Unadjusted* | *Adjusted to U.S. Concepts* |
| 1970 | 0.7 | 0.5 | 2.5 | 3.0 |
| 1971 | 0.8 | 0.7 | 3.4 | 3.8 |
| 1972 | 1.1 | 0.9 | 3.7 | 4.2 |
| 1973 | 1.2 | 1.0 | 2.6 | 2.9 |
| 1974 | 2.6 | 2.1 | 2.6 | 2.9 |
| 1975 | 4.8 | 3.9 | 4.1 | 4.9 |

Since the war it is clear that the United Kingdom has not been as successful in maintaining full employment as West Germany – and equally not as successful in sustaining economic growth. In particular the stop-go cycle has been more marked in the UK than in Germany. The United Kingdom has been even less successful than Sweden (see Table 7.II or Norway both of which countries by any definition have sustained full employment. Three of the reasons for the success of these countries in this field are a) the existence of a highly skilled, mobile labour force with an immense interest in training and re-training b) the use of subsidies to sustain jobs in potential downturns and c) the growth of public sector employment. The UK needs to look to all three policies in relation to its own future.

*Problems behind the figures*

The unemployment figures only show a snapshot of unemployment at any one time. Every year, come boom or slump, some 4 million or so people come on the unemployment register and a similar number off. Every month there is a flow of 300,000 plus onto the register and off the register and the unemployment figures rise and fall according to marginal shifts in the flow. Equally there are another 4 million or so who change jobs every year without going onto the unemployment register at all. So in total we have a situation of 8 million or so people

**Table 7.VIII:**
**Unemployed over 8 weeks and over 6 months**

| | *January 1977, G.B.* |
|---|---|
| Over 8 weeks: | 1,003,905 |
| Over 26 weeks: | 541,070 |

*Source:* Department of Employment Gazette, February 1977

**Unemployed 4 weeks and under, and over 4 weeks**

| | *May 12, 1977, G.B.* |
|---|---|
| 4 weeks and under: | 196,000 |
| Over 4 weeks | 1,090,000 |

*Source:* Department of Employment Press Release, May 24, 1977

**Table 7.IX:**
**Notified Vacancies, May 1977**

| | | *seasonally adjusted* |
|---|---|---|
| Notified to employment offices | 163,608 | 159,600 |
| Notified to careers offices | 32,412 | – |

Please note: (a) these figures apply to vacancies notified to employment and careers offices, not total vacancies.
(b) some vacancies may be notified to both employment and careers offices. The two figures should not be added to obtain a total for notified vacancies.

*Source:* Dept. of Employment Press Notice, May 24, 1977

changing their jobs every year (in fact some 10 million plus P.45s [leavers tax forms] are issued each year).

Behind the flows however are serious and developing social problems which could threaten democracy itself. These problems to which we must pay special attention relate to the young unemployed (see Chapter 4) and the long term unemployed (Tables 7.VIII-IX).

# 8 The Social Contract

**National Union of Public Employees**

This chapter is extracted from NUPE's *Economic Review 1977* drawn up by the Executive Council in May 1977 for submission to the Union's National Conference.

When the Labour Government came to office in February 1974, it did so in political circumstances which were unusual in British history. It came to power at a general election called by a Conservative Government that wanted to exert its authority over the miners, and following a period when many trade unionists – including local authority manual workers in 1970 and hospital ancillary staff in 1973 – had taken industrial action to improve their wages. And it came to power on a programme that was widely considered to be the most radical commitment to structural, socialist change since the second world war.

At the heart of this policy was the commitment to bring about "a fundamental and irreversible shift in the balance of wealth and power in favour of working people and their families." And the impetus for this radical policy came from the Social Contract – the agreement drawn up by the TUC-Labour Party Liaison Committee.

It is important to recall the original form of the Social Contract envisaged in 1973. The first TUC-Labour Party Liaison Committee document on the shape of a future Labour Government's economic policy was *Economic Policy and the Cost of Living,* published in January 1973. It was essentially designed as a rebuttal of Tory economic policy and of Tory incomes policy in particular. It rejected the deliberate fuelling of inflation by the imposition of Government-sponsored price increases and it argued forcibly that trade unions could not accept a wages policy without considering wider economic and social issues:

"The present inflation has been induced and encouraged by deliberate Government policies . . . It has proceeded to introduce new and increased social charges right across the board, including dearer school meals, and much higher charges for prescriptions and dental and ophthalmic services . . . Trade unionists are as concerned to keep down the cost of living as anyone else. They do not need to be told that what matters is real wages, not paper ones. But the problem of inflation can be properly considered only within the context of a coherent economic and social strategy – one designed both to overcome the nation's grave economic problems, and to provide the basis for co-operation between the trade unions and the Government." – *Economic Policy and the Cost of Living,* 1973 TUC Report

The broad strategy set out in *Economic Policy and the Cost of Living* was that unions could not accept a wages policy that was divorced from Government action over issues such as prices, rents and social benefits. This was in line with long-standing TUC policy; but even more significant was the section entitled "Investment, Employment and Economic Growth" which set out the basis for agreed action on the broad economic policies to be pursued by an incoming Labour Government.

This policy, which made action on the *structural* problems of the British economy a major priority for a Labour Government on taking office, was highlighted by NUPE in the 1976 economic review, *Time to Change Course.* We argued that it was now impossible for a British government to deliver full employment, a reasonable rate of economic growth, an acceptable rate of inflation, and a healthy balance of payments, because the economy was so riven with structural faults that it was becoming impossible to manage it at all. Therefore, any long-term advance towards a reconstructed socialist society – or indeed any advance in the short-term living standards and in the level of public services – would have to be based on action to reconstitute the industrial base and to control that base through central government in the interests of the people.

In *Time to Change Course* we showed that there had been a net loss of 160,000 jobs in manufacturing industry each year since 1970, with less than one in three of these being replaced by the creation of alternative jobs in manufacturing industry. This had meant a continuing failure to meet the demand for goods in both the home and export markets and a spiral of decline which had reduced the tax base for the necessary expansion of the public sector. Therefore, government intervention on a massive scale was required to reverse this trend and bring the operation of industry and its production of value under public control.

It was also necessary to do this, we pointed out in *Time to Change Course* for one other vital reason. Governments could not now control the economy as they had in the 1950s and early 1960s by pressing on the accelerator and stamping on the brake through reductions and increases in taxation. The concentration of capital and the trend to monopoly which has been evident from the beginning of the 1950s has made control over the economy much more difficult for governments to achieve because of the long-term planning which many monopolies undertake; because of the ability of multi-national companies to transfer resources, prices, production and investment between countries and different regions of individual nations; and because the proportion of net output produced by monopolies has increased from 20 per cent in 1950 to over 50 per cent in the 1970s – and will increase to 66 per cent in 1980 if this process continues unabated.

These problems were recognised in the 1973 statement:

> "Underpinning all of these policies, however, must be agreed policies on investment, employment and economic growth. And the objective must be to get faster growth in both national output and in output per man . . . wages and salaries in Britain have *not* increased faster than the average for industrial countries. What *has* increased faster is wage costs *per unit of output* – a direct result of the small rise of output in Britain . . . Fundamental to the British economic problem, therefore, is the problem of *investment* and, more generally, the problem of the control and the disposition of capital. The expansion of investment and the control of capital will thus bc one of the central tasks of the next Labur Government. And this will mean the development of new public enterprise and effective public supervision of the investment policy of large private corporations. For it is these big firms which now dominate the growth sectors of the economy – to the extent, indeed, that no less than half of the nation's manufacturing output is already accounted for by the leading 100 companies, with this degree of concentration growing year by year."
> – *Economic Policy and the Cost of Living*

In the eyes of both the TUC and the Labour Party, therefore, the Social Contract concept was not primarily concerned with persuading a Labour Government to introduce certain specific reforms, such as increases in old age pensions. It was an agreement, above all else, about the kind of total economic strategy that would be pursued by a Labour Government. And the Contract could only be a reality if the structural changes were implemented, for the reasons we pointed out in *Time to Change Course.* Such a strategy, according to *Economic Policy and the Cost of Living,* would concentrate on the creation of higher economic growth, improved investment performance and the development of new public enterprise to counteract monopoly power. It is our contention that the major direction of the Government's economic policy since February 1974 has not pursued those objectives or the objectives set out in the election manifestos of 1974; as a result the Social Contract has been undermined. But, most important of all, the Government has not begun to tackle the basic structural faults in the economy which are at the heart of Britain's industrial problems.

Following the adoption of *Economic Policy and the Cost of Living* by the TUC General Council and the National Executive Committee of the Labour Party, a list of priorities was incorporated in Labour's Programme for Britain, which was endorsed by Party Conference in 1973.

The programme stated:

> "The need is for a far-reaching *Social Contract* between workers and the Government – a contract which can be renewed each year as circumstances change and as new opportunites present themselves."
> – *Labour's Programme for Britain 1973*

It is instructive to compare the priorities set out in that programme – which were intended to implement the policy options set out in *Economic Policy and Collective Bargaining* – with the policies pursued by the Government since February 1974.

*Commitment No.1* was to introduce: "Effective price control on the key items in the household budget". Since February 1974 retail prices have increased by 72.9 per cent, and there have been particularly large price increases in those items on which low paid workers spend a high proportion of their incomes: such as fuel and light, food and transport costs.

*Commitment No.2* was to introduce "especially stringent controls on food prices including the provision of subsidies where necessary." Since February 1974 the official food price index has risen by 84.8 per cent and since January 1976 alone it has risen by a staggering 25.8 per cent. Important food subsidies are being phased out as part of Government cuts in public expenditure. These subsidies, worth £409m to families in the financial year 1976-77, will be eliminated completely by April 1978.

*Commitment No.3* was "a large and immediate increase in pensions". The Government did make a big increase in pensions immediately on taking office, but the value of pensions has been undermined by inflation and the general consequences of the Government's economic policies. Money has been saved by reducing the number of upratings in social security benefits during the period of high inflation. Professor Peter Townsend, a leading authority on social security and a member of the Labour Party National Executive Committee's Social Policy Committee, has estimated that the Government saved over £500m by failing to implement a second uprating of benefits in 1976. A further cut in social security was made when the period over which upratings would be calculated was changed; by excluding part of the period of highest price inflation from its calculations, the Government reduced the increase that should accrue to social security benefits.

*Commitment No.4* was "the abolition of prescription charges, and steady progress towards a completely free health service". The level of prescription charges has remained unchanged and the increased charges made for National Health Service spectacles, false teeth and dental treatment will cost patients a total of £20m a year.

*Commitment No.5* was to ensure "fair income tax treatment for the lower paid". There has been little progress on this commitment. Tax allowances to single and married persons have not been indexed in line with inflation, and their real value at the end of the financial year 1977-78 will be lower than at any time since the Government took office. In addition, the Government have rejected TUC proposals to improve the progressiveness of the income tax system by introducing a lower rate band of tax below the present standard rate.

*Commitment No.6* was "a reversal of the Tories' tax cuts for the rich". Some individual tax loopholes have been closed, but the Chancellor has made it a specific aspect of his policy to reduce the rates of taxation on companies so that they might increase gross profits and profit margins. In November 1974, Mr Healey made corporation tax concessions to industry in respect of the taxable value of company stocks, and these were not "conditional" on any improvement in companies' performances in terms of investment and employment creation. This reduced the Government's tax base for financing the public services, thus making it more difficult to resist the pressures for reducing public expenditure. It is also part of the Chancellor's budget strategy to reduce the impact of income taxation on "middle managers". In his 1977 Budget, Mr Healey introduced unconditional and conditional tax changes which will improve the take-home pay of a married man, with two children under eleven and earning £2,000 a year, by £1.39 per week. But a man in similar circumstances who is earning £25,000 a year will gain substantially more; he will receive an increase in take-home pay of *£16.96 per week.*

*Commitment No.7* was to "repeal the Tories' Housing Finance Acts and (introduce) restraint on rents." The Government have repealed the Conservative's Housing Finance Acts, but the cuts in public expenditure have forced local authorities to increase rents by an average of over 40 per cent in three years.

*Commitment No.8* was "a big increase in the housebuilding programme", During 1974, the Labour Government planned a large increase in council house building and by 1975 the number of starts was up by 54 per cent compared to 1973. However, as part of the July 1976 cuts the Government halted all public sector housebuilding for a month and reduced the programme of council house starts from 9,000 to 6,000 per month in England during 1976, with similar cuts in Wales and Scotland. The controls reimposed on all new schemes and land acquisition will have the effect of reducing the public sector housebuilding programme to 1974 levels. One result of this situation is that in February 1977 there were 227,400 construction workers on the dole (16.0 per cent of the workforce) against 112,900 (8.2 per cent of the workforce) in February 1974.

*Commitment No.9* was to produce "fairer treatment for private tenants, including municipalisation of privately rented homes". The 1974 Housing Act took action to implement this pledge and provide the beginnings of a coherent improvement programme. But this has now been undermined by the cuts in housing. Local authorities in England and Wales had anticipated borrowing £572m in the financial year 1975-76 to improve council accommodation, but were told by the Government that they could only spend £330m. This resulted in the abandonment of many improvements.

*Commitment No.10* was to ensure the "public ownership of land". The Community Land Act has been introduced, but this falls substantially short of public ownership. The Act, together with Government instructions to councils, specifically excludes the use of the Act to promote council housing and community facilities; local authorities are now selling off council-owned land that was earmarked for public sector housing to private developers and housing associations.

*Commitment No.11* was "action to save public transport, including subsidies to hold down fares." Subsidies, which were initially increased, have been reduced and public transport is destined to become less frequent and more expensive as the cuts bite. Local authority subsidies to unprofitable bus and train routes have been cut and British Rail services have been increased in price and reduced in volume because of the withdrawal of nationalised industry price subsidies.

*Commitment No.12* was "more effective regional development policies, including effective manpower subsidies". The effectiveness of these policies has to be judged against the background of general economic policies and their effects on employment. In February 1974 there were 628,800 men and women registered as unemployed (2.7 per cent of the total workforce). By February 1977 the total had risen to 1,421,800 (6.0 per cent of the workforce). The schemes introduced by the Government have had only a limited impact on unemployment and the December 1976 cuts in public spending will abolish the Regional Employment

Premium (a manpower subsidy to employers in development areas), saving £150m in the financial year 1977-78 and a further £170m in 1978-79. One result of the government's employment policy has been to increase dramatically the numbers of school-leavers on the dole. In February 1974 there were 9,300 school-leavers unemployed; by March 1977 this had risen to 33,300 and a peak of 208,500 had been reached in July 1976. The previous highest total under the last Conservative government was 64,300 in August 1972.

*Commitment No.13* was "a massive expansion in industrial training and retraining". Progress has been made in expanding training opportunities, and the TUC has welcomed the advances made. But, as the 1977 TUC Economic Review made clear, there is still much to be done to provide adequate training opportunities to meet today's needs.

*Commitment No.14* was "greater public control of the more powerful private companies". As NUPE pointed out in *Time to Change Course,* the industrial strategy originally adopted by the Labour Party is now virtually unrecognisable. Planning agreements are voluntary, not compulsory; and the pace of implementation has been appallingly slow – after three years only one planning agreement (with Chrysler) has been concluded; investment by private companies has dropped dramatically during the recession and the Government has rejected controls over the scope and size of investment decisions. The total industrial strategy is not co-ordinated, and relies heavily on unenforceable sector level "co-operation" through the National Economic Development Office. In the absence of positive planning measures, the failure to introduce wide-ranging nationalisation measures is even more crucial.

*Commitment No.15* was to encourage the "development of new public enterprise". The funding of the National Enterprise Board remains at a low and inadequate level and the aim of ensuring a state controlled "growth company" in each of the major industrial sectors is not capable of fulfilment. Measures have been introduced to take the shipbuilding and aerospace industries into public ownership, but ship-repairing was omitted due to the opposition of the House of Lords and the controversy over the "hybridity" of the Bill. There has been no progress on the extension of public ownership to "profitable sections or individual firms", and there have been no proposals on pharmaceuticals, road haulage or construction. Limited progress has been made in the area of machine tools with the financial assistance given to Alfred Herbert Ltd. The "nationalisation" of the North Sea oilfields has left foreign multinational oil companies with very substantial shareholdings and substantial profits will find their way abroad. The proposals made in the Labour

Party Green Paper on banking and insurance have been rejected by the Prime Minister, instead of nationalisation there is a committee on the operation of the financial institutions, chaired by Sir Harold Wilson.

*Commitment No.16* was "controls on the international movement of private capital". Export of capital from Britain has continued at a high level and the Treasury has sought to explain away the significance of capital outflows by arguing that they are not a net cost to our reserves of foreign currency. But the principal objection to capital outflows is that they are running at a high level when investment in British industry is dropping in real terms and when the level of fixed capital formation is too low to sustain the regeneration of the manufacturing base.

*Commitment No.17* was the "renegotiation of the crippling Tory terms of entry into the Common Market". Recently, the Cambridge Economic Policy Group estimated that the net annual cost of the Common Agricultural Policy to the British consumer and taxpayer is between £650m and £900m per year.

*Commitment No.18* was the "repeal of the Tory Industrial Relations Act". The Government repealed the Industrial Relations Act and replaced it with the Employment Protection Act, the Trade Union and Labour Relations Act and the Health and Safety at Work Act which are of positive benefit to workers and their unions. But they contain a number of shortcomings which need to be remedied and, in many cases, the remedies have been delayed because they require additional public expenditure.

*Commitment No.19* was "real moves towards industrial democracy in the workplace and joint control of industry". The report of the Bullock Committee on the private sector concentrates attention on worker-directors to the detriment of other forms of industrial democracy; and the deal between the Liberal Party and the Government means that the likelihood of achieving agreed legislation within the lifetime of this Parliament is now remote.

These, then, are the original commitments made resulting from the first "social contract" bargain between the TUC and the Labour Party and it is apparent that the results of many of the policies pursued by the Labour Government have been at variance with the agreement between the two wings of the Movement. It is true that there has been some progress in some areas; but in others the promising advances made in the early months of the Government have been reversed and in yet other areas there has been no progress. The Government's policies have been at variance with the letter and the spirit of the original Social Contract.

These failures are not just failures in individual policy areas, which are to be regretted as setbacks to advance in those particular fields. In total they represent a failure to maintain commitment to the philosophy of the Social Contract. It would now be extremely difficult for the Labour Party to claim, as it did at the October 1974 General Election that:

> "The Social Contract is no mere paper agreement approved by politicians and trade unions. It is not concerned solely or even primarily with wages. It covers the whole range of national policies. It is the agreed basis upon which the Labour Party and the trade unions define their common purpose . . . Labour describes – as we did in our February manifesto and as we do again at this one – the firm and detailed commitments which will be fulfilled in the field of social policy, in the fairer sharing of the nation's wealth, in the determination to restore and sustain full employment. The unions in response confirm how they will seek to exercise the newly restored right of free collective bargaining."
> – *Labour Party General Election Manifesto,* October 1974.

Because the Social Contract has been regarded as a trade-off between the trade union Movement and a Labour Government, and because the Government has failed to meet the expectations it raised amongst workers when it entered into the bargain, the Social Contract has been transformed, in the eyes of trade unionists, from an agreement about economic and social priorities into a vehicle for implementing a policy of wage restraint – and nothing more.

# PART FOUR

## The Conditions for the Restoration of Full Employment

# 9 Economic Conditions

**Francis Cripps and Frank Wilkinson**

If full employment could be achieved without any institutional reforms and without harm to any other interests, everyone would be in favour of it. The need for a campaign arises because full employment cannot be achieved so easily. This paper examines the economic conditions for full employment. It aims to show which conditions can be fulfilled now, and which cannot. This should help clarify the reforms which are necessary to make full employment possible.

*Five conditions for full employment*

The economic conditions necessary for full employment in all regions of the country and among all groups of people seeking work include:

1. *Aggregate demand:* there must be sufficient spending power to absorb a full employment level of production.

2. *Productive capacity:* physical installations and business organization must exist to supply the quantity and type of goods and services which are demanded.

3. *Geographical balance:* businesses must be located so as to provide jobs in the right areas.

4. *Occupational balance:* there must be a match between job requirements and the skills and aptitudes of people who want to work.

5. *Balance of payments:* foreign transactions must be such that the £ sterling can be held at a reasonable exchange rate.

Francis Cripps and Frank Wilkinson are at the Department of Applied Economics, Cambridge University.

There is a sixth condition which many people would add to the list – that inflation of prices and money wages must not be too rapid. We do not agree that inflation necessarily prevents full employment, but will discuss this after examining the conditions listed above.

*Aggregate demand*

Keynes stated, correctly, that a sufficiency of aggregate demand or spending power, is the single most important condition for full employment. If total spending is too small, the success of any one business in expanding sales, production and employment can only be at the expense of another. Keynes also stated, correctly, that aggregate demand can be increased by the Government through the straightforward device of cutting taxes or increasing public expenditure. This remains true under present-day conditions and it is true for the world as a whole as well as for a single country.

Although aggregate demand in any one country can always be increased by tax cuts or higher government spending, an increase in aggregate demand in that country will spill over into higher purchases or imports which may make the balance of payments unmanageable. In these circumstances it is usual for the government to reduce aggregate demand in order to limit imports. Such deflation not only raises unemployment but may make the balance of payments worse in the long run by discouraging investment in industry.

A second problem, according to many economists, is that an increase in total spending makes inflation worse. They insist that spending must be held down to control inflation. In our view a cut in spending may make inflation worse. But in any case it is not acceptable to rely on unemployment as a method either for solving balance of payments problems or for controlling inflation.

*Productive capacity*

Spending power can only be translated into jobs if the physical installations and business organization exist to produce the quantity and type of goods and services which are demanded. In an economy like the UK this is the responsibility of enterprises, most of which only invest and produce if it is profitable to do so. Not all are capable of responding to demand efficiently, but this does not prevent full employment provided that demand not satisfied by one business is usually satisfied instead by another. Postwar experience has shown that industrial countries relying on this mechanism can achieve very low levels of unemployment even when the pattern of demand is complex and changeable.

In Britain the main problem is that the response of home industries to rising demand has been too weak relative to that of foreign competitors. British producers' share of foreign markets has declined while foreign producers' share of the British market has increased, causing a chronically weak balance of payments and restriction of aggregate demand. The consequence has been a fall in employment not only in the manufacturing industries which lost markets to foreign producers, but also in other sectors of the economy which suffered from the restriction of aggregate demand.

Despite the present magnitude of this problem, some believe that no reforms are necessary. They argue that with a low exchange rate for the £ sterling, with favourable tax rules, and with benefits to come from North Sea oil, British industry will now recover its competitive position sufficiently to allow a gradual return to full employment.

In our view this prospect is exceedingly unlikely. In the long term industry should be made more competitive by planned and coordinated investment and marketing. Meanwhile to permit an early return to full employment the balance of payments should be put right by direct action – i.e. by import controls and exchange controls.

### *Geographical and occupational balance*

Unemployment may in parts be 'structural' in the sense that when full employment is achieved in some areas and for some occupations there remains a pool of people seeking work in the 'wrong' areas or with the 'wrong' skills.

Without disputing the case for government training and information services, we do not believe that occupational mismatch is a major problem in times when there is an overall high level of employment. In such times job mobility is always high, work experience is easy to come by, employers have a strong incentive to provide training themselves, and unsatisfactory jobs tend to be eliminated because they are difficult to fill.

Geographical imbalance is a more serious obstacle to full employment, for which large-scale migration of people is not an acceptable remedy. Regional policy – i.e. inducements and controls to secure migration of jobs – has become the subject of competition between authorities in different regions not only of the UK but across Western Europe and even in other parts of the world. This competition might be reduced under general conditions of full employment in industrial countries. But some form of regional policy will still be essential and to be fully effective it may have to be coordinated at an international level.

*The balance of payments*

If there was no balance of payments problem the Government could reflate the economy by tax cuts and extra public spending on the scale necessary to restore full employment. The reasons why full employment causes balance of payments problems are that a higher level of aggregate demand in the UK means greater expenditure on imports and that exports (and other sources of foreign exchange) are not nearly sufficient to pay for 'full-employment' imports.

Trade deficits are potentially very damaging because they make sterling insecure. The Government has little power to defend sterling because of the level of Britain's short-term indebtedness and the Government's commitment to free trade and capital movements. For these reasons, when there is a balance of payments deficit a collapse of sterling can only be prevented by international support. The terms imposed as conditions for such help mean that the British Government does not have independence in its economic decision making.

The usual remedy for balance of payments deficits, and the one insisted on by the IMF and other creditors, has been to make sure that total spending is held down to a level at which people and businesses do not choose to buy too large a volume of imports. Since 1956 the British Government has repeatedly had to cut total spending in order to limit imports, even though this meant reducing aggregate demand further and further below the level required for full employment. Since 1973 the same process has been at work in other industrial countries, causing a general world recession.

The remedy for the balance of payments problem favoured by some economists – devaluation of the exchange rate – has been shown by experience not to be a practical one. It is supposed to make British goods cheaper in world markets, thereby raising exports. The problem is that the response of exports is weak and slow, while devaluation accelerates inflation in Britain so that any initial competitive advantage is soon reduced or lost. To make devaluation 'work' it would be necessary to enforce strict wage control for a long period while profits increased by very large amounts.

All methods for removing the balance of payments obstacle to full employment are at present prevented by one or more powerful interest groups. Devaluation cannot be made effective because organized workers are able to prevent a very large, permanent increase in profits at the expense of wages. Import controls are prevented by pressure from other governments and from international companies. Vigorous planning to make UK industry more competitive is blocked by the refusal of corporate management to allow intervention in its decision-making.

Full employment will only be possible if this stalemate is resolved one way or another.

*Inflation*

If the balance of payments could be controlled directly, inflation would not be an insuperable obstacle to full employment. At present inflation makes full employment more difficult to achieve in two ways. First it makes sterling less atractive as an investment currency and therefore weakens the balance of payments. Second, it leads to a clamour against reflation on the argument, which influences governments even though (as we believe) it is a false argument, that inflation is caused by deficits in the Government's budget.

Provided only that sterling was not weakened, full employment would reduce inflation by making a much larger flow of production available out of which the competing claims of wages, profits and finance for public expenditure could more easily be met. Certainly full employment must strengthen the bargaining position of workers and could therefore increase money wage settlements. But as against this, real wage and living standards would be higher so that the intensity of inflationary conflict might be reduced. Moreover a high level of job opportunities and of opportunities for businesses to expand sales would make it easier for wages to be improved by increases in productivity.

Inflation has a political as well as an economic aspect. Whether there is full employment or high unemployment, inflation can only be held down if the conflict over income distribution is resolved partly by political means as well as by industrial bargaining.

*The strategy of a campaign*

To reduce unemployment urgently, any campaign must focus on reflation and on measures to deal with the balance of payments. To reduce unemployment fully and permanently, the campaign must extend to the reform of business organization and of regional policy.

One lesson of the past two decades is that improved trade union organization and workers' rights in direct bargaining with employers have failed to fulfil crucial objectives in regard to jobs and real wages. But on the other hand, experience has shown that the government finds it extremely difficult, if not impossible, to impose solutions on the labour movement without rank and file acceptance. The struggle for full employment certainly cannot be won by fragmented industrial action. It must be organized on a local, national and international basis because the two most important issues are government budgetary policy and the balance of payments. The failure to maintain post-war full employment has been a political failure with respect to both these issues.

# 10 Technological Unemployment

**Michael Barratt Brown**

Michael Barratt Brown is Senior Tutor in Economics at Sheffield University.

It is beginning to be fairly widely appreciated that the number of those employed in Britain in manufacturing industry is 1½ million less than it was ten years ago and the decline in mining and agriculture accounts for a reduction of about another half million. Yet the working population as a whole, including the unemployed, is now half a million more than in 1966. A million extra jobs have been created in local and central government services since 1967 but we still have a million more unemployed than in that year, and the situation would be worse still if many thousands of young people were not staying at school and even more old people and women had not retired earlier from the labour force than they might have wished to.

It is sometimes argued that, if more capital were invested in industry then employment prospects would improve. I think they well might, because the competitiveness of British industry would improve, exports would increase and the economy could be permitted to operate at a higher general level of activity without the problem of a gigantic deficit in our foreign trade balance which I consider in Chapter 11.

But I do not believe that such investment would create any new jobs in manufacturing or mining or agriculture or even in transport and distribution and the public utilities (gas, electricity and water). Capital stock in manufacturing industry including plant and machinery nearly doubled in the period 1963-1976 while employment was cut by 15%. We should have more workers at work in the construction industries after the present slump and in private services, but the bulk of any increase would come from being able to employ more in public services. The simple fact is that new investment in productive industries, including transport and distribution, and in finance and commerce too, now reduces rather than increases employment opportunities. To take examples: The British Steel Corporation plans to increase output in its Ten Year Development Strategy by 50% with a work force reduced by 20%. The government "Think Tank's" estimate for the British car industry is that even if output were raised by 50% to 1.9 million cars a year by 1985 this would mean 55,000 fewer jobs than in July 1975. The effects of the introduction of computer control and completely automated production processes into industry are only just beginning to be felt in Britain. But from the results of the most modern Japanese and American plant introduced into Australia, which is being used as a testing ground for many new processes, several conclusions can be drawn.

*The New Technology*

1. Labour savings are far beyond anything experienced since the first industrial revolution. A new automated textile mill introduced in Britain in 1968 halved the employment requirements per unit of output of a conventional mill by reducing mainly the semi-skilled and unskilled grades of workers. These requirements have been halved again by new plant introduced in 1976, this time by reducing mainly the skilled and administrative grades.

A plant is reported to be making all the beer cans required by Australians with just 24 full time workers and 12 other part-time workers to meet the needs of South East Asia. No maintenance staff is employed; the computer reports when parts will need replacing and sub-contract staff are called in for a day to effect the replacement.

The cash desks at supermarket stores are now connected to a computer centre so that all sales are recorded by article and the computer carries out a regular stock taking and reorders stock that is running low. Most of the office and clerical staff have been dismissed and even the cash desk girls are employed in full only at peak shopping hours.

2. Part-time and casual employment and labour-only sub-contracting have become widespread, replacing full time employees even in traditional full time jobs like motor car assembly. Many of these part-timers are women and immigrants working shifts and especially night shifts when clerical work and stacking has to be done in stock yards and supermarkets.

Ford of Australia has one third women employees on its assembly lines and nearly half of all its workers were born outside Australia or U.K.

Forty girls in one of the tax offices on shifts have replaced 780 men and women working by day. The computer is fed by them and in return it measures and records how much work the girls have done by quality as well as quantity during their shift.

3. Automated and computer controlled plants are being established by transnational firms with the most advanced machinery not in the developed countries but increasingly in underdeveloped countries and regions. These plants make use of unemployed graduates and unskilled labour both of which can be obtained at much lower rates than in developed countries. This kind of industrial development is encouraged also by government finance, tax concessions and subsidies and by government provision of communications and transport services; and is made possible by the absence of the need for maintenance staff or other local technological services, lack of which in the past had proved an obstacle to the location of modern plant in underdeveloped economies.

An Australian boot and shoe manufacturer, offspring of a transnational company, is now established in Singapore with Japanese plant and local labour, and has been undercutting all Australian manufacture.

Oil refineries of transnational companies based in Singapore and operated by local labour are now supplying much of the Australian market. The skilled work of controlling the plant is "in the hands" of one black box made in Japan and costing only a few hundred dollars.

Recent heavy investment by transnational companies in the USA might seem to contradict these trends. But this is explained by the employment of illegal immigrants in the Southern States who are estimated (conservatively) to total 9 millions.

*The Transnational Companies and the New Technology*

The new technology that has just been described is not simply to be bought in the market by any little company that is interested anywhere in the world. Some of it is on licence at high rentals, subject to patent laws. Most of it is available only through the direct operations or subsidiaries of the giant transnational companies. This fact has important implications for the governments, trade unions and working people of all countries. The power of the giant transnational companies lies not only in their size and omnipresence but in the monopolistic positions they can establish in the new technology that they research and develop. The products of these innovations are sold at super profits until they are copied or rivalled or supplanted by their competitors, who will also be giant transnational companies. It is a battle of pikes in the fish pond, the smaller fish are steadily devoured and now the pikes are at each other's throats.

The power of the transnational companies over the new technology has far reaching implications for national measures to protect employment. These companies, in order to survive in world competition, must make their decisions on timing and location of investment without consideration of the interests of any particular country including their own country of origin. Their movements of capital and of goods and their transfer pricing policies are indeed extremely difficult for any national government to control. It is sometimes argued that even successful national state measures to maintain full employment in the past were only effective at the expense of other nation states to which the unemployment was exported. But this is not necessarily so. If each nation state government seeks to maintain a high level of economic activity to sustain full employment, all will benefit. And this can be true even where governments of states whose economies have fallen behind others in competitiveness protect their industries (by tariffs and other barriers to imports), so long as the overall activity in their economies is as a result of protectionist measures, kept at a level higher than it would have been without such protection. What most seriously reduces world trade exchanges is not so much government controls imposed upon imports as the general deflating policies adopted by governments to balance their foreign trade.

Of course, if all governments abandon full employment policies, or find them increasingly difficult to maintain because of the operations of the transnational companies, whether they impose tariffs and import controls against each other as in the 1930s or deflate their economies, as they do today, the effect will be equally disastrous. Economic activity all round will be reduced and unemployment will soar. This is what happened in 1975. Without international agreements on maintaining full employment and on permitting protective measures to be adopted by less competitive trade partners, world trade and world economic activity declined and unemployment in one country multiplied as it spread throughout all others. The danger is that the process tends to be cumulative, especially where the decisions on investment are made quite opportunistically by the dominant transnational companies. This works in two ways:

On the one hand, nation states like Japan and West Germany whose industries have established a competitive lead in several fields of foreign trade do not need to deflate their economies to balance their trade exchanges as much as others like Britain and Italy (not to mention the Third World) whose industries have fallen behind. Higher rates of activity encourage investment in new technology in the one, lower rates of activity discourage investment in the other. The gap widens, as it has done over a long period of time between the developed and underdeveloped economies.

On the one hand, governments of nation states, with increasingly *un*-competitive industries, which attempt to correct this growing imbalance by stepping up state employment can only do so by raising taxes, probably to a level higher than in the states with more competitive industries. The transnational companies, however, prefer to invest where taxes are low. The only way for the poorer countries, then, to attract their investment, is by tax concessions and by lower wages and so larger reserves of unemployed labour. And the new technology provides little new employment and, in fact, as we have seen, tends to reduce employment opportunities. Britain thus, shares many characteristics of an underdeveloped economy.

The fact is that there is no alternative for governments facing technological backwardness than to step up state spending (1) on their own development of the advanced technology that the transnational companies are denying them, in so far as this is necessary to balance their foreign payments and meet the needs of their people for consumer goods; (2) in public services which are labour intensive and maintain full employment. The two must go together; neither should be seen as in some way an alternative to the other.

### *Trade Union Defences against the Transnational Companies' New Technology*

The operations of the transnational companies as vectors of the most advanced technology in the capitalist world system present problems of control not only to the governments of nation states but equally to the national trade unions. The internationalism of the industrial working class was born in the shape of the First International as a defence against the use by employers of unorganised foreign labour to break the strengthening organisation of their own workers. Levels of technology and productivity were not at all dissimilar in all capitalist countries in the 1860s and 1870s. The political aspirations of the unions were limited to legal and political recognition within their own nation states. Trade union solidarity was in the interests of all, to win union recognition and to defend employment and rising living standards in the industrialised capitalist states.

Today, the international solidarity of the workers in the transnational companies is all the more necessary than it was a century ago. The less well-organised are used to weaken the better organised. Shifts of investment are threatened by the transnational companies as weapons to break the effectiveness of industrial action, as in the threat of Henry Ford II to switch investment out of Britain during the 1970 strike. But now that the unions have won national recognition and legal status, they tend to look to national protection rather than to international action for the defence of their livelihood. Moreover, two vast gaps have opened up inside the ranks of the workers – the one between the technology and productivity in the advanced sector of the transnational companies and what obtains in the rest of industry everywhere; the other betwen the standards of living of workers in the developed economies and in the underdeveloped economies. The possibility for the giant companies of dividing and conquering is infinitely greater.

While the centre of capital accumulation has increasingly moved from national centres of finance and industry to the giant transnational company, so the centre of trade union power has moved – especially in Britain – from national trade union offices to the joint combine committees of shop stewards. The writ of these committees does not, however, run beyond the borders of the nation. If there are no effective international government agreements to control the power of the giant companies and maintain full employment, still less are there any effective international agreements between unions. World Union Councils have been established by the ICFTU for a number of transnational companies, especially in the motor car and chemical industries. These have been concerned mainly to exchange information about wages and conditions and about major plans for transferring production. They have not been used in any way to coordinate government and company employment policies.

The only large scale attempt at such coordination was the abortive joint TUC and Labour Government proposal for Planning Agreements with large UK companies pressed forward by Tony Benn as Secretary of State for Industry in 1974-75 and subsequently abandoned. A small scale attempt was made by the English and Italian shop stewards of Dunlop and Pirelli after their merger in 1972. The joint demand was made for investment by the merged company in new job opportunities in place of the jobs lost by rationalisation. Barriers of language and organisational structure make such joint action at company union level extremely difficult; but, if it could be combined with action at international government level, there is no doubt that the combination could be very effective. It is often argued that one of the advantages of joint action by governments through the EEC is that the giant European companies can be more effectively controlled thereby and that the European trade unions can be involved in this control. There has been little or no sign of any such control being exercised despite much discussion of the problem, and the fact is that the influence of the European Trade Union Confederation on EEC policy making has been slight enough; while its influence on company policy has been nil. Until union power at the level of the company and government power at the level of the nation can be combined and coordinated country by country, the transnational company's power to divide and conquer nations and unions will continue and the result will be a persistent or worsening condition of employment and economic activity at levels well below what is possible.

*New Jobs for Old*

It has already been made clear that, desirable as it is to overcome the tendency of the transnational companies to create conditions of less than full employment, there is no solution to be found through creating more jobs in manufacturing, or in mining, transport or distribution. New investment, however much it is needed, will reduce and not increase the number of jobs. It is quite false, however, to argue from this that we must accept much lower levels of employment. Not only are there great opportunities in the new labour saving technology for reducing the length of the working day and working week but there is a vast range of services, and especially of public and social services, where automation is inappropriate and human needs remain to be met.

Projections were made by the Department of Employment in 1975 for employment changes up to 1981. These suggested continuing contraction of employment in agriculture, mining, and manufacturing; relative stability in construction, transport and distribution and a major expansion in public and private services, comparing 1981 with 1973 the last year of relatively full employment. The figures given were as in Table 10.I with estimates for 1976 added. All figures include employers, self-employed and employees.

Even taking into account that some of the projected changes between 1973 and 1981 had already taken place by 1976, it can be seen that alongside the declines still to come, especially in agriculture and mining, there were increases expected in the public services. The most disturbing element in these projections is that all and more of the decline in

**Table 10.I: Employment by Industry in Great Britain**

*Actual figures for 1973 and 1976 with Projections for 1981*

*(all figures in thousands)*

| *Industry* | *Mid 1973 Actual* | *Mid 1976 Estimate* | *Mid 1981 Projected* | *1981 Projection Compared with 1973 Actual* |
|---|---|---|---|---|
| **Production and distribution** | | | | |
| Agriculture | 640 | 610 | 540 | –100 |
| Mining | 360 | 340 | 270 | – 90 |
| Manufacturing | 7950 | 7450 | 7650 | –300 |
| Construction | 1870 | 1770 | 1840 | – 30 |
| Public Utilities | 350 | 330 | 370 | + 20 |
| Transport | 1540 | 1500 | 1560 | + 20 |
| Distribution | 3240 | 3200 | 3140 | –100 |
| **Private Services** | | | | |
| Finance, Insurance, etc. | 1040 | 1090 | 1240 | +200 |
| Other Private & Domestic | 3200 | 3190 | 3230 | + 30 |
| **Public Services** | | | | |
| Health | 1040 | 1190 | 1340 | +300 |
| Education | 1510 | 1760 | 1910 | +400 |
| Other local and central government | 1790 | 1900 | 2010 | +220 |
| Total | 24530 | 24330 | 25000 | +470 |

*Source:* Department of Employment *Gazette*, May 1975 and July 1977

Note: The fall in employment from 1973 to 1976 of only 200,000 conceals an increase in unemployment by 700,000 because the potential working population rose by 500,000 over these years as a result of rising birth rates in the 1950s.

manufacturing employment expected between 1973 and 1981 had already occurred by 1976. Of course some has been the result of deliberate deflation by the government and might be corrected in a new upswing of demand. The sharp drop in construction would certainly be corrected. But all that we have seen of the likely results of new investment in manufacturing industry suggests that this will be actually labour saving. The implication of these trends is that even larger increases in public employment will be needed than are shown in the Table if something near full employment is to be reestablished. Instead of another half million jobs in the public services perhaps as many as twice that number will be required by the early 1980s.

The idea that in some way the country cannot afford such an increase is the result of a total confusion which has been propagated in the last few years by some economists and taken up by some government ministers. What the country cannot afford is to meet the consumer needs of the population, including an increasing number of service workers, from imports which are not paid for by exports. To increase exports and/or reduce imports does not, however, depend on switching workers back from service employment into production. It depends on investment in new plant and equipment which will produce goods at prices that are competitive with those we now import. Such plant and equipment, as I have insisted throughout this contribution, will need fewer and not more workers not only for the same volume of output but for even larger volumes.

This is the essence of the new industrial revolution through which we are now moving. It is an extraordinary reflection of the failing powers of capitalism that the prospect of reduced employment in meeting the basic needs (and many of the luxuries) of our lives should arouse fear and resistance. That we should have the opportunity not only of easier work and shorter hours but of a far wider range of public, social and cultural services might be supposed to be a blessing. There is no doubt that it could still be a blessing – and not only for those who live in the rich developed economies but for the world's poor. It will require, however, a major effort of socialist organisation to ensure that the increasing wealth accumulated in a few giant industrial companies spreading across the whole world is fed back all the time to meeting the needs of the people.

# 11 International Aspects

Michael Barratt Brown

In open economies, determined primarily by private capital accumulation and only secondarily by Government management, the level of employment that can be sustained depends on the foreign balance of payments. Any particular level of economic activity and employment implies a level of demand for imports by industry of machinery and raw materials and by consumers of food and manufacturers. These have to be paid for by exports of goods and services or by borrowing. There are limits set to borrowing not only by the expectations of the lenders but also by the costs of repayment plus interest charges, since these must act as a drag on growth in economic activity. In order to reestablish full employment in Britain by the 1980s, that is to reduce unemployment to half-million *and* absorb the 150,000 new workers each year arising from the high birth rates of the 1960s, it has been estimated that a growth rate of 5% a year is required for a decade. That is twice the rate achieved in Britain in the past; and the cause of slow growth rates in the past has always been the balance of payments constraint.

*Competitive Decline of British Industry*

Whenever in the past decades in Britain the full employment target has been achieved and economic activity rose to a high level, then imports tended to flood in which could not be paid for by exports; and the Government had to cut back expenditure and raise taxes and interest rates to get the country's foreign payments in balance again. But such deflationary policies had the long run effect of raising prices and checking new investment, so that British industry tended to become less and less competitive in world trade. Increased imports were more and more difficult to cover with increased exports. To sell British exports the value of the £ sterling was allowed to fall, but this only raised the price we had to pay for imports.

Governments in countries like Britain and Italy that have strong Labour movements could not pass the main burden of deflation onto the workers, so that profits were cut into and investment was still further checked. The Government could prevent the growth of unemployment by increasing its own expenditure. But unless exports rose to keep up with imports, the balance of payments deficit grew and borrowing from abroad had to be stepped up. Britain and Italy were caught in a vicious spiral of rising prices and declining competitiveness along with the underdeveloped countries, while Germany and Japan (and France and the USA to a less extent) enjoyed complementary virtuous spirals of growth and increasing competitive strength.

The following Table illustrates the story:

**Table 11.I: Comparative Industrial Competitiveness. Capitalist World 1967-76**

| *Industrial Output (index)* | *U.K.* | *Italy* | *France* | *West Germany* | *Japan* | *USA* | *All OECD* |
|---|---|---|---|---|---|---|---|
| 1967 | 90 | 85 | 80 | 74 | 66 | 93 | 84 |
| 1970 | 100 | 100 | 100 | 100 | 100 | 100 | 100 |
| 1976 | 104 | 108 | 124 | 112 | 125 | 120 | 120 |
| *Share of Trade in Manufactures (%)* | | | | | | | |
| 1967 | 12.3 | 7.0 | 8.5 | 19.5 | 9.8 | 20.4 | 100( 70) |
| 1970 | 10.8 | 7.2 | 8.7 | 19.8 | 11.7 | 18.5 | 100(100) |
| 1976 | 8.7 | 7.1 | 9.8 | 20.6 | 14.6 | 17.3 | 100(156) |

Note: The last column in brackets shows the volume increase in world trade based on 1970=100.

## *The World Slump*

Behind the failing competitiveness of British industry there lies the slowing rate of growth and actual stagnation of the capitalist world economy. Growth rates of output and world trade averaging 7% and 10% a year in the late 1960s have fallen to half these figures and less. Table 11.I shows the declining rate of growth in the six years after 1970 compared with the three years before. There are two obvious elements in this crisis and a third that may lie behind them both. First, there is the growing challenge of German and Japanese industry to the dominant position of the USA – a challenge that led to the ending of the reign of the dollar as the world's currency and to all the subsequent uncertainties of floating exchange rates. Second, the long industrial boom led finally to shortages or threatened shortages of primary products – fuels and raw materials and foodstuffs. The result was a sharp rise in prices not only of oil but of many other minerals and agricultural products (especially coffee, cocoa and tea). This movement in the terms of trade against the industrial countries and in favour of primary producers was a sharp reversal of a long trend the other way.

**Table 11.II: Export Prices of Manufactured and Primary Products, 1968/70-1976**

| *Year* | *Manufactures* | *Food* | *Non-food Agric.* | *Minerals* | *Oil* |
|---|---|---|---|---|---|
| 1968-70 (Av) | 100 | 100 | 100 | 100 | 100 |
| 1971 | 111 | 104 | 94 | 96 | 122 |
| 1972 | 120 | 118 | 117 | 98 | 137 |
| 1973 | 141 | 164 | 205 | 132 | 182 |
| 1974 | 172 | 252 | 211 | 180 | 643 |
| 1975 | 193 | 226 | 177 | 164 | 641 |
| 1976 | 194 | 243 | 208 | 172 | 688 |
| 1977 (April) | 206 | 388 | 231 | 185 | – |

These figures may not appear immediately relevant to the maintenance of full employment. But for Britain alone the rise in the price of imported raw materials between 1972 and 1974 was the equivalent of a 25% deterioration in the terms of trade and that amounted to a cut of 6% in the national income. The Labour Government borrowed the money and tried to avoid much of the cut by expanding the economy in the hope of obtaining a corresponding rise in exports. But other Governments of industrial countries took the cuts on board; and, at the same time the primary producers and especially the oil producers, failed to spend all of their newly gained wealth. So world trade declined in 1975 leaving Britain exposed to rising imports and falling markets for exports. More borrowing was needed and the IMF stipulated public expenditure cuts for 1977-8 just when world trade was expanding again and balanced home and export growth was not only possible but essential to take up the unemployed.

Lying behind the uneven development of the giant capitalist powers and of industrial and primary production, some experts descern a more deep seated cause of capitalist crisis, which has much graver implications for employment. This is the cumulative effect of the growing concentration of productive activity in a few giant capital intensive plants which by use of computers and automation can enormously increase output without employing any more workers, often in fact reducing employment. Output per worker in such productive work rises far beyond the average and with it the monopolistic profits of the giant companies and potential wage increases for their workers. The remainder of the workers can enjoy no such productivity increase and find decreasing opportunities for productive employment.

Governments find themselves faced with the more and more difficult task of transferring wealth by taxation from the profits and wages in the ever narrowing monopolistic capital intensive high productivity sector in order to finance employment in the rest of the economy. In economies like those of West Germany and Japan the problem is in part solved by a great expansion of exports, but this only worsens the problem in those economies like Britain and Italy which are taking in as imports the West German and Japanese exports. Capital is transferred from countries with high taxation and low growth to centres of growth and relatively lower taxes. The uneven development of national economies is only aggravated by Government measures that hold back capital accumulation for growth, but growth is only possible within balance of payments constraints.

*Import Controls and State Investment*

The moral of the story of the British economy in the last three decades is that, while economic activity and full employment do depend in the long run on maintaining a balance of exports and imports, that balance cannot in the long run be corrected by reducing employment and economic activity at home to encourage exports and reduce imports. Such stop-go methods only worsen the situation. And yet something must be done to check imports and encourage exports when they get out of balance. The alternative to 'stop-go' is much more direct control over the economy through import controls and state investment. Instead of checking the whole growth of the economy and deliberately creating unemployment in order to reduce imports and allow exports to catch up, discriminatory restrictions are imposed temporarily on imports. At the same time, state funds are applied to investment in new and more efficient plant to produce for export and also for home demand in place of those imports like machinery and manufactured goods which can be replaced by home production. There is a growing list of goods which British industry once supplied but for which we now depend increasingly on imports. Motor cars are not the only example – just the most obvious.

It is quite wrong to suppose that food and raw materials are now Britain's major imports or the ones that have grown fastest in recent years. Table 11.III shows just how wrong:

**Table 11.III: U.K. Imports by Volume and Shares 1970-76**

| | *Food Beverage Tobacco* | *Fuels* | *Materials* | *Semi-Manufactures* | *Finalised Manufactures* |
|---|---|---|---|---|---|
| 1976 Import Volume Index | 101 | 87 | 93 | 150 | 200 |
| 1970 = 100 | 100 | 100 | 100 | 100 | 100 |
| 1976 Share in Total Imports (%) | 16 | 18 | 10 | 27 | 29 |
| 1970 Share (%) | 23 | 11 | 15 | 28 | 23 |

The trend shown in the Table had been going on long before 1970, and must be corrected if full employment is to be achieved again. Why then have these alternative policies not been applied?

Arguments against the use of import controls are that other countries will retaliate and all trade will suffer, ours as a major trading nation among the worst. But other countries have imposed import controls without retaliation and, since others know that retaliation will harm them too, the general dangers are less than are supposed. Of course, the individual companies like Toyota and Sony and Volkswagen and Peugeot will scream for action from their governments. Nobody wants a full scale trade war, however, and all will hope that the restrictions will be shortlived. The other argument is that firms that are protected by import controls will be the last to do anything to improve their competitiveness.

This is where the element of state investment comes in to complement the import controls. Firms can be encouraged to improve their competitiveness and increase their capacity to meet expanding home and export demand by the offer of state funds. The urgency of this cannot be exaggerated. The growth of economic activity implied in achieving full employment by the 1980s will require a massive increase in capacity. Workers cannot work without having machines to work with and buildings to work in – and that goes for teachers and Health Service workers as much as for those in productive industries.

Arguments against state investment come from two sides. On the one side, it is said that this is feather-bedding and waste of tax payers money, and it would be better to reduce taxes and let profits grow. In fact taxes on business have been heavily cut in Britain in the last few years through grants and tax concessions. But there has been no increase at all in private fixed investment in plant, machinery, buildings etc. since 1970. Much of the capital available for investment in Britain has gone overseas in the transnational operations of Britain's giant companies. Table 11.IV reveals the figures involved: the increasing proportion of private investment overseas and the failure of investment at home to rise after 1970.

**Table 11.IV: U.K. National Product and Private Investment at Home and Overseas 1967 - 1976**

*(All figures £m at 1970 prices)*

| *Year* | *G.D.P.* | *Private Sector Fixed Investment (excl. Dwellings)* | *Private U.K. Investment Overseas* |
|---|---|---|---|
| 1967 | 40,416 | 3,772 | 456 |
| 1968 | 41,904 | 3,948 | 727 |
| 1969 | 42,600 | 4,316 | 679 |
| 1970 | 43,488 | 4,504 | 789 |
| 1971 | 44,588 | 4,588 | 836 |
| 1972 | 45,284 | 4,748 | 1,383 |
| 1973 | 48,000 | 5,208 | 1,848 |
| 1974 | 48,064 | 5,092 | 1,149 |
| 1975 | 47,400 | 4,812 | 1,377 |
| 1976 | 47,852 | 4,616 | 1,923 |

On the other side, it is said that state funds are being used to prop up capitalist exploitation without any adequate strings being attached to ensure that the public interest benefits. This is the crux of the matter. The concept of the Labour Party's Planning Agreements was designed precisely to ensure that public funds were used to promote the public interest.

Since the greater part of Britain's foreign trade – both imports and exports – are now the result of movements *inside* the giant trans-national companies, agreements between governments and companies on the balance of exports and imports *inside* these companies is likely to be much more effective than the imposition of import controls. There is no doubt that fear of the potential effectiveness of such agreements, which could be publicly monitored, led to the virulent campaign of private industry against Tony Benn who advocated them, and was as a result replaced by Harold Wilson at the Department of Industry by a less determined character. Planning agreements combining import controls and the leverage of the availability of state funds for investment on prescribed conditions remain the most effective device available to Governments for managing the balance of payments in order to secure the economic growth necessary for full employment.

### *Britain and the EEC*

Even to propose import controls and state subventions for British industry under Planning Agreements as an alternative economic policy to reestablish full employment is to run foul of the provisions of the

Common Market for ensuring 'fair competition'. Free movement of goods, and of capital and labour also, lies at the very heart of the Common Market philosophy. Only in the case of agricultural products is the free market replaced by a planned market designed to guarantee prices for European farmers that will protect them from competition in any other part of the world. In manufactured goods the leading West Europeans have the competitive edge on the rest of the world; they need no protection. Britain as a member of the EEC gets the worst of both bargains in Europe – higher than world prices for her large scale imported agricultural products and a highly competitive market for her manufactured exports which must be sold in Europe to pay for imports.

Those Parliamentarians of the Left in the Labour Party, supported by Tony Benn, in the Common Market Safeguards Committee, have taken the first step to challenge the bargains reached in the past by the original Western European states in the Market. The challenge is crucial if balance of exports and imports is to be achieved so that full employment can be reached in Britain by the 1980s. Apart from the diversion of Britain's trade towards increased exchanges inside Europe, which Britain must challenge if economic growth for full employment is to be restored, there is the challenge involved in the concept of Planning Agreements supported by state funds. Common Market rules governing the competition between member states lay down that state funds shall not be used to subsidise economic activities except in regions where heavy unemployment already exists. Threats to future employment prospects can only be countered through application of the quite limited social funds of the EEC. This is only available where the Market's own policies have caused distortion or where major disturbances have already occurred.

### *Towards an Alternative International Economic Policy*

The argument of this paper should have demonstrated that full employment cannot be reestablished in Britain without balancing the overseas payments on imports and exports of goods and services, taking also into account the capital movements of the giant companies by means of transfer payments. It is no good supposing that these matters can be negotiated at a plant or company level without involving the power of the state influenced by a major growth of public investment and the power of the unions in cementing and monitoring the deal. But the power of the state, we have just suggested, is subject to the limitations of EEC ground rules. The time has come for these to be challenged.

What is needed from the Labour Government at the present juncture (June 1977) is that import controls and state investment incentives should be combined with a programme of long term trade agreements with major trading partners. The aim of these would be to underpin the balance of exports and imports so that a more rapid rate of economic growth can be sustained and full employment can be thus steadily established. It is not too late to make this change of policy and rescue the tarnished image of the Labour Party. But it soon will be too late not only to rescue the Labour Party but to rescue the British economy. But it is necessary to repeat what was said at the beginning of this paper, that full employment and high levels of economic activity depend upon maintaining a balance of exports with imports. To do this requires physical controls over the economy, however much they challenge the rules of the EEC.

The British economy cannot be rescued without creating a new framework of foreign trade capable of sustaining the growth in employment. Above all it must be emphasized that the balance of payments cannot be left to be corrected by increasing exports of oil from the North Sea. For one thing the question arises concerning the situation when the oil supply reached its maximum rate of flow and begins to decline. Even more important is the question of correcting Britain's present industrial decline and excessive dependence on imports for such a high proportion of the machinery and manufactured goods we use. The North Sea oil and gas only provide a bonus which makes possible the necessary investment in new productive capacity without our having to hold back the growth of consumption to make way for extra exports to pay for imported oil as well as for the new investment. To fail now to use this brief opportunity to make good the long years of neglect of Britain's productive capacity will be something our children and grandchildren will not easily forgive us.

# 12 'Socially Useful' Work

**Mike Brown**
**Tony Emerson**
**David Griffiths**

Mike Brown is a member of the Trade Union Committee for International Co-operation and Development.

Tony Emerson is Secretary of SERA, The Socialist Environment and Resources Association.

David Griffiths is Secretary of the Labour Campaign for Nuclear Disarmament.

*Introduction*

The Full Employment Appeal rightly points out that "Most of the major social and democratic advances which have been made in Britain since 1945 have been directly founded upon the fact that relatively full employment has prevailed for almost three decades", and that consequently, "full employment remains a key political priority". We have no quarrel with either the analysis or the objective.

There is a danger, however, that the debate will be concerned solely with the number of jobs available, and with sharing available employment through such measures as earlier retirement, shorter hours, less overtime and more prolonged full-time education. Important as these issues are, arguments about the *quantity* of employment must in our view be complemented by a debate about the *quality* of employment – about *what* is produced and *how*

*Changing what we produce*

As well as our present mass unemployment, we also have massive *malemployment.* We reject the facile argument that all production is socially useful, because the fact that something is produced means that there is a demand, and therefore a need, for it. It is clear that, in the context of an inegalitarian market economy, and even more so in the context of international inequalities, 'need' and 'demand' do not coincide.

Thus 'aggregate demand' has more than doubled since the war, but much of the increase in production has met 'unneeds': military production, luxury goods (from Concorde to centrifugal salad-dryers), goods designed not to last, and over-elaborate or over-packaged goods. At the same time real needs remain unsatisfied, even in the developed world – e.g. for food of the right quality, for transport for the non-motorised majority, for adequate housing, heating and so on. And beyond that are the immense unmet needs of the third world. These are the needs of people who cannot make their needs felt as 'effective demand' in the national and international economic system because of inadequate purchasing power.

We believe, therefore, that a socialist employment strategy must take as its starting point the meeting of needs, not the creation of 'demand' in the abstract.

*Three examples*

It is no abstract argument that the labour movement must increasingly be concerned with *what* is produced, and not just *how much*. A whole range of challenges is developing to our present priorities of production, which the labour movement ignores at its peril. Our organisations are concerned with three of those challenges – the challenges of development, disarmament and the environment. They are, surely, three of the most fundamental challenges that the world faces, and they each pose an *apparent* threat to jobs. But in fact, as we argue below, in tackling each of the issues there is the potential for more employment, not less.

*Development*

The oil price rises of 1973-74 heralded a new era in relations between the third world and the industrialised countries, and their echoes continue to resound in the various forums of the 'North/South' dialogue. Fundamental to the changed situation is the demand of the non-aligned nations for a New International Economic Order, and central to the NIEO is the demand for a changed international division of labour. Third world countries are concerned to escape their present role as suppliers of commodities to the industrialised world, and increasingly to take on the role of processing those commodities into manufactured goods themselves.

The primary development need of most third world countries is for employment. Consequently the massive increase in their manufacturing output which is contemplated – the target of the non-aligned countries is to increase their share of world manufacturing output from its present 7% to 25% by the year 2000 – will be primarily in labour-intensive industries such as textiles, footwear, timber products and processed foods. The challenge which this poses to employment policies in the industrialised countries is very evident already in, for example, the high level of import penetration in textiles.

Yet beyond the short-run conflict between the employment needs of workers in the rich and poor worlds – seen in the demands for import controls on the one hand, greater access to rich world markets on the other – is the prospect of a new interdependence, and of immense new export opportunities for industrialised countries as the purchasing power of the third world expands. To respond to third world demands, however, and to realise that new interdependence, will require changes in the pattern of production in the industrialised countries.

*The environment*

A huge range of issues falls under the loose label 'the environment', and few of them have yet been adequately considered by the labour movement. But it is clear that some of our industries are based on levels of consumption of finite raw materials and energy which cannot be sustained indefinitely even if the rich world continues to pre-empt the lion's share of natural resources, and certainly cannot be sustained if global resources are to be shared more equally. Take the question of energy policy. In our view the economy cannot be based on an indefinite expansion in the use of fossil fuels and nuclear energy, which will meet both resource constraints and fundamental physical barriers. This view will be widely perceived in the labour movement as a threat to jobs – witness the intensity of the campaign to bring forward the order for Drax B, and the widespread support (for example from both the TUC and the Labour Party) for the fast breeder reactor, despite its grave implications for health and safety, industrial relations and civil liberties.

Take transport policy. Constraints on oil supplies mean that our transport policy cannot continue to centre on increasing use of the private car, certainly in its present form. Yet hundreds of thousands of jobs are directly and indirectly dependent on the car industry.

Take the question of built-in obsolescence. The production of throw-away or short-lived goods is unacceptable wasteful of scarce resources – yet it is also a source of employment.

Once again, however, the short-term threats contain a long-term promise. The nuclear industry, on top of its other disadvantages, produces a tiny number of jobs for an immense capital investment – it is, perhaps, the least effective method of job creation yet devised by capitalism. Moreover, the energy it produces will be used to automate other workers out of jobs. The alternative, sustainable sources of energy, on the other hand, are vastly more labour-intensive. So would be a national insulation programme to reduce energy requirements. So too are the recycling and re-use industries on which a less wasteful use of natural resources depends, while the manufacture of products designed to last is likely to demand more skill than, for example, a car assembly line turning out vehicles designed for obsolescence.

*Disarmament*

The arms industry is perhaps the prime example of an industry which provides employment on a substantial scale, yet cannot be regarded as geared to human need. Disarmament may not be an immediate 'threat', certainly under the policies of the present Labour Government, which has increased military expenditure in real terms alongside cuts in many of the public services. But the labour movement must reckon with the possibility that peace might one day break out.

Less need be said here, perhaps, than in the other two cases, since the dilemma is a more familiar one. The labour movement has long campaigned for reductions in military spending, yet the limited steps which governments have taken along that road have often been resisted by trade unionists immediately concerned because their jobs were directly threatened.

But it is equally true in this area that the threat to jobs masks an opportunity. For the arms industry absorbs skilled labour, technical expertise and research and development effort to a disproportionate extent – all resources which could be redeployed towards the meeting of human needs. It is an extraordinary comment on the divergence between needs and demand that – to paraphrase a comment in the Lucas Aerospace workers' corporate plan – technology can provide a nuclear missile accurate to 30 metres over intercontinental distances, but is not used to provide the urban heating systems which would prevent pensioners dying from hypothermia during a British winter. Moreover the arms industry, like the nuclear energy industry, is exceptionally capital-intensive, so investment in peaceful technologies would provide *more* jobs not less.

In each of these three cases, policies which would contribute to meeting human needs are apparently in conflict with the need for full employment. Certainly the objectives of development, disarmament and respect for the environment cannot be secured if we insist on preserving every job in every industry in our present distorted economy. Yet in each case, too, the short-term threat masks a long-term promise of *more* jobs not less, if we can find ways of realising that promise.

*The quality of work*

So far we have considered a number of reasons why, if human needs are to be met, there must be changes in the pattern of *what is produced.* One fundamental human need, however, is for meaningful work, and we believe that the *quality of work* must be the second starting point for a socialist employment strategy.

Much of our present unemployment, of course, is cyclical, reflecting the deep recession in the capitalist world economy. But much is also structural, or technological, unemployment. The increasing capital-intensity and energy-intensity of production – which we have noted in the energy and arms industries – has two consequences for workers.

First, the substitution of capital for labour has reduced the demand for manufacturing labour as such. The expansion of public services has compensated to some extent for this, but not fully. The potential benefits of technological change have not been spread equally among the remaining industrial labour force, as they could have been through, for example shorter working hours. Instead, the big corporations have reaped the benefit, as the only agencies with sufficient capital for modern large-scale production, while a large group of people has emerged who get work only irregularly, if at all. Heavily over-represented among them are the under-25s, immigrants, the disabled and married women. These groups are largely unorganised and politically powerless, so much so that their lack of employment is not regarded as a major political problem. Often they are the same groups whose needs are not registered as 'effective demand'.

For these groups, clearly, the quality of work is inadequate. They are likely to have no work at all, or to be open to exploitation in the Grunwick style. But the second problem arising from increasing capital-intensity is that, for all but a few technological workers, the growth path of capitalist production involves minimising the use of *skilled* labour.

As well as looking afresh at the priorities of production, therefore, we believe the labour movement needs to examine the concept of 'intermediate' technology. Intermediate technology aims to avoid the extremes of back-breaking drudgery on the one hand, and giant automated plants on the other. It aims to design machines which *make full use of human skill,* while automating out the monotonous and dangerous work. Some research into intermediate technology design has already been done in the paper, soap and other industries. Such research should also aim to 'design in' safety and 'design out' pollution, to reuse waste products, and to minimise the use of raw materials and energy. The labour movement should be demanding more research and development in this direction, as part of a programme for tackling unemployment.

### *Corporate plans*

At an abstract level, the issues we discussed earlier – development, disarmament and the environment – are evidently inter-related. Perhaps the most exciting feature of the corporate plan produced two years ago by the Lucas Aerospace Combine Shop Stewards Committee, which must by now be well known throughout the labour movement, was that it brought the various issues together in concrete terms, within an aggressive trade union strategy for extending the limits of collective bargaining.

Lucas Aerospace is substantially dependent on military work. In the corporate plan, the Combine Committee proposed a number of alternative products of greater social utility which would reduce this dependence ('disarmament'). They included sustainable energy systems ('environment') and transport and other technologies appropriate for use in the third world ('development'). Central to the whole exercise was a fuller use of human skills – on the one hand the corporate plan included products which would themselves make full use of their operators' skills; on the other, it was based on an assessment of how the skills already possessed by Lucas Aerospace workers could themselves be fully used.

With the Lucas initiative, issues which had hitherto been the preserve of the diarmament, development and environment 'lobbies' seemed suddenly to be on the agenda of mainstream trade unionism. There have not yet to our knowledge been any further initiatives to compare with the Lucas workers' 1200-page plan. But there *have* been more limited initiatives, or at least discussions, in a number of other companies. Significantly, these have been in just those sectors which we have identified as being vulnerable – arms (Vickers, BAC, Rolls-Royce), cars (Chrysler), power stations (Parsons, Clarke Chapman), textile machinery (Scraggs).

### *A framework of planning*

The development of corporate plans, of proposals for alternative, socially useful production, is crucially dependent on grass-roots initiatives by the workers directly concerned. Such initiatives are not enough, however. The Lucas workers have encountered unresolved problems in pursuing their strategy, which can perhaps be most simply summarised by recalling that the corporate plan has yet to be implemented.

The missing link is any response from the Government. The similarity between the corporate plan concept and the Labour Party's concept of a planning agreement is obvious. Through effective planning of industrial conversion, a Labour Government could ensure that the social costs of industrial change were not borne wholly by the workers concerned, as they are in a market economy. Without such a framework of planning, workers do all too often face a choice between malemployment or unemployment, and a preference for the former is entirely understandable.

Among the many tragedies of the present Government's record, one of the most significant in any long-term perspective is surely that the planning powers which would permit an effective response to third world aspirations, environmental realities and the demand for disarmament have been left in cold storage.

*A full employment strategy*

An effective system of economic planning must be at the core of any strategy for full employment. But other steps are also important:

First, we need selective increases in purchasing power to enable unmet needs to be registered as 'demand'. This requires greater equality both nationally and internationally, and increases in public expenditure to enable community provision of unmet needs (e.g. public transport, district heating schemes, environmental health measures).

Second, as we have outlined already, we need greater research and development of 'appropriate' technologies – appropriate in the products they make, the kind of jobs they provide, and the resources they use. Alongside this, a logical trade union demand would be for technology that uses more skilled labour.

Third, we need greater public sector support for a whole range of industrial experiment. The number of workers' co-operatives is steadily growing, for example those set up in Meriden, Kirkby and Fakenham, and more recently in Skelmersdale and Milton Keynes. Wandsworth and Fife councils have been encouraging this development on a local basis – an example which could be followed elsewhere. Similarly, there is scope for the expansion of municipal enterprise.

Fourth, we need greatly increased investment in training and retraining. Changes in what we produce and in technology both demand new skills, while co-operative enterprises create a need for training in a whole range of management skills.

Fifth, there are the obvious measures: shorter hours, less overtime, and earlier retirement. We put these last not because they are unimportant, but because our aim has been to emphasize that the debate on full employment must be about *what* work is done and *how* it is done, not just about *how much* work there is. For the same reason we have not discussed demands for general reflation of the economy (though we would comment that a strategy based solely on indiscriminate increases in investment is likely, under the present economic ground-rules, to mean *less* jobs not more). Full employment *is* crucial, both because it forms the basis for other social advances and because the right to work is a basic human right. But the right to *socially useful* work must also be put on the agenda.

'Revolutionary' purists may argue that it is a demand which cannot be taken seriously until we 'achieve socialism'. We would put the argument the other way round. Is not the demand for socially useful production at the core of the socialist critique of capitalism? Will it not put some flesh on the often rather abstractly proclaimed superiority of 'planning' over 'the market', if we stop talking only in macroeconomic aggregate and begin to talk about what *specifically* would be different about production organised for social need? Is it not concrete demands of this kind which are likely to capture the imagination of working people and draw them into the socialist movement? And would not such demands, if backed up by mass public support and political action, be very hard to contain?

The labour movement in a capitalist society has a vital and indispensable defensive role to play. But if we are seen *only* to defend the sectional interests of existing workers in existing industries, if we are seen to be protecting our own jobs at the expense of denying third world aspirations, squandering natural resources and perpetuating the arms race – and at the expense of those excluded from regular work altogether – then we will be seen increasingly as part of the problem, and not as the key to the solution.

# PART FIVE
## Remedies

# 13 The 35-Hour Week

John Hughes

There could not be a better time to go over to the 35 hour week. Not only in Britain but in other major industrial economies.

Modern technology in manufacturing means that even with major increases in the stock of productive capital and major increases in output, there is only limited scope for employment to increase – if actual working hours do not fall. This is particularly true for manual workers. In Britain the manufacturing capital stock grew nearly 40 per cent between 1965 and 1975 while the total hours worked by "operatives" (manual workers) *fell* 24 per cent. A recent article on the Federal Republic of Germany (in the Department of Employment Gazette, April 1977) says:

> "In spite of the gradual lifting of the recession unemployment levels are expected to remain high in the Federal Republic because of rationalisation in industry. This is, in effect, reducing the number of jobs available and increased investment tends to be geared towards further rationalisation rather than creating more jobs."

Given the size of public sector financing deficits in many major economies, and further efforts by the authorities to curb such deficits, it is unlikely that further large increases in public sector employment will be forthcoming – if working hours do not fall.

Yet the number of people seeking to enter the labour market continues to grow. The age structure is such that particularly large and still increasing numbers of young workers are seeking jobs. (In England and Wales the annual number of school-leavers was 620,000 ten years ago, is now over 750,000, and is expected to rise to above 810,000 by 1979/80.)

The latest unemployment figures for European countries (mainly for spring 1977) are sombre. France and Germany, with registered unemployment near one million, have already experienced over two years of unemployment at such high levels. The United Kingdom figure has more than doubled its unemployment since 1974, and a seasonally adjusted level of one and a third million has persisted since mid 1976; most expert forecasts anticipate further increases in UK unemployment. The latest date for Ireland and Denmark show unemployment as 12 per cent of the total number insured. The sample survey in Italy showed unemployment over three-quarters of a million from the second quarter of 1976 onwards. (The North American figures reveal an unemployment rate there of over 7 per cent of tht total labour force.) There is clearly serious danger of "structural" unemployment persisting at high levels in 1977 and after, particularly for young workers, and not least in the case of Britain.

Those resisting the possibility that a reduction in the normal or "basic"[1] working week could contribute positively to restoring full employment argue somewhat contradictorily that it would be damagingly inflationary, and that it would not have much impact on employment because employers would counter by reorganisation of work to increase productivity.

On previous experience, a major and widespread reduction in working hours, without loss of pay, has *not* been the cause of a major increase in unit costs. Part of the "cost" is likely to be offset by higher efficiency; part by the greater willingness of organised labour – in return for the shorter week – to settle for moderate advances in weekly pay. That seems to be the lesson of past hours reductions. At the same time an increase in employment required in the economy *is* created. This is the more obvious if actual hours fall more or less in line with the reduction in normal hours. Here, too, earlier experience suggests that a fall in actual hours does occur, and with more joint planning of manpower and control of overtime this effect could be enhanced.

It can be shown that on reasonable assumptions, a phased transition to the 35 hour week could in Britain have a larger effect in reducing the present mass unemployment and avoiding long period unemployment[2] than any other measure or combination of economic measures that has been proposed. Assuming the employment effect were 40 per cent of the total change in basic hours, the full transition to a 35 hour normal week in Britain would create about 750,000 jobs, nearly 400,000 of which would be for manual men (who represent the highest unemployment rate). Probably this would mean a reduction of half a million or slightly more in registered unemployment. Depending on the bargaining approach adopted, this might be largely achieved within two to three years.

Previous post-war reductions in hours of work were launched in periods of high economic activity, and involved more problems of costs and employment than would a planned move to the 35 hour week in 1977-79. Even so they were managed without undue strain. The 35 hour week, pursued *now,* would offer a strategy to return to full employment; without that, the British "industrial strategy" through which the government aims at the strengthened development of productive industry is incomplete and unbalanced.

But the critics of the 35 hour week raise the danger of damage to our comparative cost position, the danger of weakened competitiveness. The right answer to this from the British trade unions is to recognise the need for – and the opportunity for – a massive exercise in trade union solidarity and co-ordinated action internationally. This can prove in practice the reality of a European trade union movement. Through the European TUC, and through direct contacts with particular European trade unions and TUCs, we must raise the challenge of achieving a 35 hour week across the continent – and beyond; not as aspiration for the future but as a practical programme for today. It was as long ago as 1935 that the ILO came forward with the 40 hour week objective. Over 40 years later it is the right time to ask the world labour movement to take the next major step forward.

### *1. Earlier Reductions in Hours*

The previous reduction in normal hours in Britain brought hours down from 44 to 40 in two stages. Most of the fall from 44 to 42 was concentrated in the years 1959 to 1961; the reduction from 42 to 40 was mainly bunched in 1964-66. In each period the official index of normal hours for manual workers fell by 3.7 per cent.

At the time the fall in "actual" hours was less pronounced in 1959-61 (1.9 per cent) but continued into 1962. Economic activity was rising strongly in 1959 (so that cyclically "actual" hours would have been likely to rise with increased overtime being worked); by 1960-61 there there was a very high level of activity and a low level of unemployment, but a recession developed in 1962. In the circumstances it is interesting that hours actually worked fell as much as they did. In 1964-65 labour market conditions were similar to those of 1960-61 – a low level of unemployment which may have encouraged firms to maintain actual hours as normal hours fell. But the year 1966 saw a recession developing and a more marked reduction in actual hours worked.

The years in which reductions in normal hours were concentrated were not the most suitable in another respect. 1960-61 were years of very limited increase in labour productivity; so were 1964-66. This is typical of British experiences of "peak" and immediate post-peak years in the trade cycle. Consequently there was little productivity to offset the rise in unit labour costs caused by the shortening of normal hours. (From this point of view the best timing for a major reduction in normal hours is immediately after the recession stage of the trade cycle; for the first years of resumed economic expansion are most favourable to a high rate of increase in both labour and capital productivity.)

Even so, neither of the two previous periods of reductions in normal hours caused any noticeable problems of accelerated cost of inflation. In 1959-61 income from employment per unit of output rose just over 7 per cent; this was distinctly *less* than in the equivalent years in the previous trade cycle (1954-56) when no hours reduction occurred. In 1964-66 wages and salaries per unit of output rose by 9½ per cent across the economy; this compares very favourably with the steeper rise (nearly 15 per cent) in the equivalent years of the following economic cycle when no hours reductions occurred. Thus, despite the timing of the reductions in hours in relation to the trade cycle making it more difficult to achieve direct cost savings, there is no evidence that pay costs (per unity of output) rose faster than they would have done had there been no reduction in normal hours.

Although many other factors are involved, it is useful to note that in the recessions in the British economy following each of the sets of years in which reductions of normal hours occurred, the unemployment peak remained below 600,000. By contrast, in the two most recent trade cycles, in neither of which has there been a reduction in normal hours, unemployment peaks moved very much higher (to over 900,000 in 1972 and over 1.3 million in 1976-77).

Over the longer term the fall in actual hours has been more closely in line with the reduction in normal hours. The official index of actual hours of operatives in manufacturing industry shows a fall of 9.5 per cent between 1956 and 1974 (these years occupy equivalent positions in terms of the trade cycle). We should discard the myth that if normal hours were reduced actual hours would not respond and overtime would rise.

The last major official analysis of hours of work, overtime, and shift-working in Britian was a National Board for Prices and Incomes Report in 1970. (Though each year there is a statistical survey.) This report was not able to draw on any very extensive studies of the effects of reducing *actual* hours, but it did report some interesting experience from France.[3]

In the French case, following the industrial unrest of 1968 a number of agreements with provisions for limiting overtime and reducing actual hours were concluded. Late in 1969 a survey was made as to the effects of the reduction in actual hours. Among those firms that had reduced hours the average reduction was 3.4 per cent; the loss of production attributable was only a little over a third of that. Among the industrial firms reducing hours of work 48 per cent hired more labour and 27 per cent introduced or extended shiftwork (the shiftwork extension was more noticeable among larger firms).

Perhaps the lessons of this recent British and French experience might be summarised as:

1. A reduction in normal hours is associated with some reduction in actual hours.
2. Reduction in actual hours *in the short run* would be more pronounced where there is still considerable unemployment and additional labour can be recruited; in the longer run, the fall in actual hours is likely to be as great as the fall in normal hours.
3. Reduction in actual hours could also be tackled by collective bargaining on manpower policies setting limits to overtime, etc. (It would be important both for employment creation reasons and to reduce cost inflation to prevent reduced normal hours leaking away into increased overtime working.)
4. A substantial part of the reduction in normal and actual hours might be handled by firms without major loss of production (i.e. there would be sizeable efficiency gains).
5. A fairly high proportion of firms would hire more labour as part of the process of adjusting to reduced working hours. A considerable number of firms would also seek to extend shiftworking in such a context.

### *2. Background Analysis: Basic and Actual Hours in Britain*

The British pattern of normal and actual hours differs from that in other countries in two respects. (1) In Britain normal hours for non-manual workers are generally below those for manual workers. (Whereas on the continent the 40 hour week is widespread for both manual and non-manual categories.) (2) The majority of leading countries have laws which lay down normal and/or maximum hours of work and provisions covering the working of overtime as well. This is not true of Britain, in general, though some degree of protection applies to certain categories (juveniles and women workers in some circumstances; transport drivers).

The New Earnings Survey (Table 13.I) shows the overall position for Britain in 1976 (for full time workers).

**Table 13.I: Basic and Actual Hours worked, 1976**

| | *Basic Hours* | *Over-time* | *Total Hours* |
|---|---|---|---|
| Manual men | 39.9 | 5.4 | 45.3 |
| Manual women | 38.5 | 0.8 | 39.3 |
| Non-manual men | 37.2 | 1.3 | 38.5 |
| Non-manual women | 36.2 | 0.3 | 36.5 |

It is obvious from the table that only in the case of manual men is overtime a significant element. As for non manual workers, their basic hours are already more than half way (measured from 40 hours) towards the 35 hour week.

Consequently:

- Only limited further change in working hours is needed to bring non-manual workers to the 35 hour week.
- This contrasts to some extent with the situation in other countries where the scale of adjustment involved for non-manual workers would be greater.
- Differences in normal hours have been one of the elements of differentiation in Britain between manual and non-manual workers; therefore, to reduce hours to a *common* level (such as 35) would imply the reduction of this hours differential.
- The main scope for reducing both normal and actual hours is concentrated on manual men. It is on this occupational category that most unemployment is concentrated: on the last official figures just over 60 per cent of male employees are manual, but manual workers account for over 80 per cent of male unemployment (nearly three quarters of a million male manual workers registered as unemployed).

To measure more exactly what would be involved in reducing normal hours, it is helpful to look in more detail at the pattern of normal hours in Britain (Table 13.II).

**Table 13.II: The Distribution of Basic Weeks**

*(Full time workers. Percentages relate to each occupational category, i.e. each column sums to 100)*

| *Basic Week* | *Manual men* | *Manual women* | *Non-manual men* | *Non-manual women* |
|---|---|---|---|---|
| Up to 35 | 1.7% | 16.8% | 20.7% | 30.8% |
| Over 35, up to 38 | 10.7% | 13.5% | 54.1% | 47.4% |
| Over 38, up to 40 | 81.2% | 67.6% | 19.7% | 20.6% |
| Over 40 | 6.4% | 2.1% | 5.5% | 1.2% |

Factors which may be noted:

a. Around half the non-manual labour force is on a basic week of between between 36 and 38 hours.
b. Only a fifth of non-manual workers are on or near a 40 hour week, this contrast with two thirds of manual women and over four fifths of manual men.
c. Some 30 per cent of non-manual women, 20 per cent of non-manual men, and one sixth of manual women are already working a 35 hour week or less; but this applies to very few manual men.

Using the detailed information available from the New Earnings Survey enables an accurate estimate to be made of the proportionate reduction in basic hours required to reach a 35 hour week *for all workers presently above that.*

– For manual men an average reduction of 12%.
– For manual women an average reduction of 10%.
– For non-manual men an average reduction of 7%.
– For non-manual women an average reduction of 6%.

Over the whole economy (and estimating for juveniles, as well as allowing for part-time workers whose hours would be unchanged) the reduction in all basic weeks in excess of 35 hours to no more than 35 hours would require an average reduction of 8.7 per cent in basic hours.

It would, however, be very unrealistic to translate this statistic into an assumed increase in employment required. That unreality could be put as follows: if there were *no* changes in output, *no* changes in productivity, *no* changes in overtime worked, then the 35 hour week in Britain would require a 9½ per cent increase in employment. This point only serves to indicate the importance in reality of influencing accompanying changes in productivity, and in overtime. It suggests that phasing a major reduction over two or three years may be important; it should be noted that the labour force in Britain is expected to expand to the early 1980s.

The statistics so far presented have concentrated on "normal" hours. But it is helpful also to know about characteristic features of "actual" hours worked. From the New Earnings Survey the following relevant facts stand out:

i. Very large numbers of workers do work actual hours at or very close to their normal hours. In the latest survey over half of all full-time employees were working actual hours per week in the range of 36-40. This is not merely a feature of non-manual work.

Over half of manual women workers were working actual hours of 39-40, and so were a third of manual men.

ii. The proportion of manual men working very extended hours has already been falling in the 1970s, despite the lack of any change in their basic weekly hours. In 1970 28 per cent worked over 50 hours, in 1975 this had fallen to 21 per cent.

iii. It might have been expected that shift workers would tend to work to a shorter actual week as some compensation for the social and other disadvantages of shift work. In fact 23 per cent of manual men received shift premia. But 58 per cent of them worked overtime and those that did work overtime averaged 10½ hours overtime in the survey period (these figures are slightly higher than for manual men generally). It might be argued that shift-workers could claim some priority in the reduction of both normal and actual hours of work.

This brief survey does suggest that both reductions in normal hours would be quite widely transmitted into reductions in actual hours, and that bargainers would need to consider both dimensions of the working week – "normal" and "actual" hours of work.

*3. A Possible Strategy and its likely Effects*

In order to evoke a sharper discussion of the real economic and organisational issue involved in a planned and co-ordinated reduction in the normal week, the following section sets out the basis for a feasible plan of action. The approach is designed to minimise any economically harmful "costs" of the reduction in the working week. But even more imperatively it is designed to help remove the scourge of persistent and excessively high unemployment in 1980.

i. On the basis of constructive collective bargaining and support from related economic, manpower, and fiscal policies, the objective should be to reduce the basic working week in Britain to 35 hours in 1980.

ii. This programme could be thought of as involving two stages – the first of which would reduce normal weeks to 37/38 hours (for many bargainers this might naturally appear as 37½ hours) and the second to reduce normal hours to 35.

iii. The first stage of such a programme would in total involve approximately *half* the proportionate reduction in normal hours (and associated requirement for increased employment) set out above, for the complete transition to the 35 hour week. But its effects would be disproportionately important for manual workers.

Reducing normal hours to 37 a week would involve a fall of nearly 7 per cent in the basic week for manual workers, but only around a 2 per cent to 2½ per cent fall in basic hours for non-manual workers. The second stage would affect manual and non-manual workers more or less equally.

iv. The approach should not be concerned to maintain existing differences in normal hours as between manual and non manual workers. But studies of work requirements and arrangements might be needed in a number of cases when determining what constitutes the recorded working day and working week (miners and teachers might be examples of the need for such studies).

v. It would be helpful if the phasing of agreements for reduced normal weeks were subject to TUC guidelines. This is particularly relevant if other elements of TUC guidelines (such as the rule involving a 12 month interval between settlements) persist.

vi. The target should be set for each bargaining unit of offsetting one-third to one-half of the cost of the transition to the 35 hour week by improved practices and overall increased efficiency. The one-third yardstick might be more appropriate where equipment, etc. remains substantially unchanged; the one-half target where improved equipment etc. could enhance performance. The context of bargained reduction in the working week would enable constructive "productivity bargaining" to go ahead in a way which it can hardly be expected to in the present context of mass unemployment and unchanged hours of work.

viii. The bargained agreements should include provisions for monitoring and joint regulation of overtime and for avoiding any general in overtime working beyond its previous levels. It would be helpful if special surveys were made of firms or industries where a significant number of manual men are working excessive overtime.

ix. There should be particular attention to reduction of both normal and actual hours in the case of shiftworkers. This might include more widespread provision for giving time off in lieu where overtime (or overtime beyond an agreed level) has been worked.

x. It would be reasonable to ask the state to assist the creation of additional employment through relevant fiscal policies. The state has an interest in the employment creation that could be set in train by a reduction of both normal and actual hours; each worker removed from the unemployment register and put to work represents a reduction in public expenditure on unemployment benefit and an increase in public revenue from taxes on earned income.

The state would also wish to avoid the "leakage" of the potential employment effect of reduced hours into higher levels of overtime because these would be more cost inflationary than employment of additional workers. It would make sense, therefore, for the state to *reduce* the cost of reduced hours to employers, *and* to increase the net employment resulting, by some type of subsidy to additional employment – financed from the improved fiscal balance resulting from that employment. This could help to steer the employer away from increased reliance on overtime working towards additional recruitment.

xi. Most productive industries are currently operating with a great deal of surplus capacity. (In its last survey the Confederation of British Industries found two thirds of firms working below normal capacity.) Consequently, on previous trade cycle experiences, if there is renewed and sustained growth of industrial production in 1978-79 high rates of improvement in both capital and labour productivity should be forthcoming in production industries. This should mean both that the reduction in normal hours need not prevent the attainment of high rates of economic growth (if other aspects of national economic management make that possible), and that there is still more reason to believe that rising productivity would substantially offset increases in unit costs that might have been associated with the reduction in normal hours.

xii. It would be important for the TUC to ask other trade union centres to achieve a broadly similar advance to the 35 hour week. This could act on a world scale to tackle the mass unemployment that has emerged. It would also mean that the transition to the 35 hour week would not be delayed by employer and government resistance based on fears of adverse effects on the competitive comparative cost, position of any one country.

### *4. Assessing the Potential Employment Effect in Britain*

Some indication has been given as to the potential scale of the employment that might be created as a result of a programme for reducing the length of the normal working week. Necessarily, any such projections must be somewhat arbitrary at this stage, until much closer empirical investigation of particular sectors and methods of reducing hours has been conducted. But it is useful to explain the kind of reasoning behind the estimates put forward here.

A balance of factors is involved.

Firstly, it is assumed that there would be a considerable offset to the cost of moving to reduced normal hours as a result of enhanced efficiency. People may work more efficiently within the reduced working week, companies may be stimulated to improve methods of work organisation and to re-tool. Firms may be able to take up elements of current slack or under-employment. These productivity gains would reduce the costs involved in the hours reduction but also the additional employment required.

Secondly, some part of the change to shorter working hours may simply mean a loss of production (this might be true in certain services). It might be argued that some slight loss of production could be involved if there were an adverse effect on competitiveness.

Thirdly, there might in the short run be some tendency for overtime working to increase. Some of the proposals made in the previous section were concerned to minimise this overtime "leakage". We have seen that the problem is mainly one concerning manual men rather than the other categories in the labour force.

As a first approximation it is suggested that 60 per cent of the employment effect that it would result if *nothing* changed except normal (and with them, actual) hours could be absorbed from some combination of higher productivity, reduced output, and increased overtime. It is not necessary to identify the exact contribution to this offset to the employment effect caused by each of the three factors (e.g. it could be 40 per cent, 10 per cent, 10 per cent, respectively; or 35 per cent, 10 per cent and 15 per cent).

The employment estimates are based on a further simplifying assumption. This is that all normal weeks longer than a given number of hours are reduced to the stated number. In practice the industrial world may not be so tidy, and the process may be incomplete. But, on the other side, some groups may succeed in reducing their normal hours even below the "target" figure postulated.

On this basis employment effects in terms of "full time equivalents" can be estimated for the British economy. In practice the total employment effects would be expected to be larger than the figures to be given below because many of the additional jobs created would be part-time (e.g. in the distributive and other service trades).

*Phase 1.* Coming down to a 37 hour basic week for all workers whose basic week is at present longer than that would increase employment by some 360,000. Over 60 per cent of the extra jobs created (about 220,000) would be for manual men. Registered unemployment might be expected to fall by over 250,000.

Rather depending on the balance of the three offsetting factors mentioned above, the "cost" of phase 1 might be something like 3 to 4 per cent increase in labour costs. But this is assuming no reduction in pay for the basic week, and no reduction in general pressures to raise bargained pay for the basic week. The former is realistic, the latter is probably exaggerating the total cost push of trade unions under conditions of a general bargaining of reduced normal hours.

*Phase 1 and 2.* The normal working hours are brought down to 35 for all workers with longer hours of work. This would create about 750,000 additional jobs; nearly 400,000 for manual men. Registered unemployment would be expected to fall by half a million. The scale and occupational balance of these figures suggests the relevance of the 35 hour week goal as a way of reducing the massive unemployment that disfigures the economy. The increase in labour costs associated with a general reduction to the 35 hour normal week might be 7 per cent. It has already been noted that this is on fairly harsh assumptions about the complete maintenance of trade union pushfulness on the basic weekly wage. This paper earlier assumed that this effect would be spread across some two to three years.

It is time to turn the 35 hour week from a slogan into a practical strategy. This paper is a contribution to the debate that is needed.

FOOTNOTES

1. "Normal" and "basic" are used inter-changeably in this article.
2. On the last count, for January 1977, over 20% of the registered unemployed in Britain had been unemployed for over twelve months. The comparable figure for the Federal Republic of Germany (for September 1976) was over 18%, nearly double the proportion that had been unemployed for over a year some twelve months earlier.
3. National Board for Prices and Incomes, Report No.161, Pages 45-46.

# 14 Three Modest Proposals

John Hughes

**Proposal 1** *"Two for One" Grant Aided, Half time work for men aged 63-64.*

a. The present "job swop" scheme appears to be attracting little support from employed men aged 64+ (only 14,000 by July 1977). This may reasonably be related to the considerable gap between weekly earnings for those in full time work, aged 60+, and the £23 benefit originally offered (raised to £26.50 in August 1977). The 1976 NES showed £59 average gross weekly earnings for manual workers aged 60-64; even "lowest decile" earnings were fractionally above £40 a week.

b. The attraction of the scheme might be very much greater if what was offered was a grant supplementing half time work (for workers presently working full time). In what follows it is, for purpose of convenience, assumed that the grant offered might be £11.50 (i.e. half the £23 originally offered).

c. Let us suppose that the provisions of the scheme would be satisfied if,

   i. Two men currently working full-time and aged 63+ went over to half time work;

   ii. The arrangements were jointly monitored by the appropriate trade union representatives and the employer;

   iii. The employer hired one additional full-time worker currently on the unemployment register. (The scheme could be compatible with "normal" overtime being worked – shared between the two men – though this would increase the need for monitoring.)

d. Assuming that weekly earnings for the 60-64 age group are currently about 12 per cent higher than at the time of the April, 1976 NES, average weekly earnings of manual men might be around £66. Lower quartile earnings might be around £54 to £55. The value to the worker of the combined package of half-time work and grant would depend on whether the grant were subject to tax.

e. Assuming first of all that the grant was free of tax, then its gross pay equivalent value would be over £17. Looking at it in gross pay equivalent terms the "lower quartile" manual worker would suffer only a reduction of £10 a week in gross pay terms as a result of dropping to half time work. The post-tax comparison would be even more favourable (though of course it would vary with household composition), and on fairly simple assumptions net (post-tax) pay might fall no more than about £6 a week. Even if we shift to consider how such a scheme would affect a worker with average weekly earnings for the age group (c. £66 for a manual man), the gross pay equivalent would be around 75 per cent of full time earnings, and the net (post tax) comparison would be around 80 per cent or slightly higher. To a worker near retirement this might look an attractive exchange for half time work.

f. It could also be argued in support of such a scheme that it offers an important new opportunity for workers to adjust from full-time work to retirement, by coming down to half-time work for a bridging period of up to two years. This might assist greatly in personal adjustment, development of leisure interests, etc.

g. It is not clear whether employers would need to be "induced" to co-operate in such a scheme. One way to do so would be to offer some grant (or waiving of National Insurance liabilities) related to the employment of men from the register in place of workers going over to half time work. This would be particularly justified where the employer took up a worker who had been on the register for a long period (say, six months or more).

h. The scheme could, of course, be made regionally selective and/or occupationally selective. It would make sense to develop it in the first place in relation to manual men in areas of high unemployment.

i. An increasing number of manual men are covered by industrial pensions schemes. It might be worth considering how far arrangements could be negotiated with specific industrial pension funds (e.g. those for particular nationalised industries) to generate similar "package" offers at a similar nominal cost to the Exchequer by an agreed revision of pension fund retirement terms, (e.g. suppose pension entitlement at age 65 is a proportion of terminal earnings, these could be based on age 63 earnings inflation adjusted or on some other formula). This approach would, of course, have to be agreed by the relevant trade unions. Encouragement of industrially suitable arrangements for half-time bridges to retirement might thereby emerge in a flexible way.

j. It is assumed throughout, that the scheme offer is so far as workers aged 63+ are concerned essentially voluntary. Hence any pension fund arrangements would have to incorporate the principle of voluntarism.

k. A scheme on the above lines might be relatively cost-effective to the Exchequer (given the revenue gain and expenditure reduction involved in removing men from the register). It could also be designed to be selective so as to tackle particularly high levels of "structural" unemployment in particular labour markets (regional and/or industrial).

l. In principle it would not be difficult to withdraw from such a scheme if conditions in the labour market improved. This withdrawal might be selective or general. If the idea of a two-year part-time "bridge" to retirement proved attractive to both employers and labour, the results of the scheme could be subjected to research monitoring; potentially a 64-66 "bridge" could be offered alongside the fixed 65 retirement age in the longer run.

*Footnote:* The "half time" formula might in some cases be better applied and be more in the interests of the workers concerned – as an alternation of 2 and 3 days full-time work in succeeding weeks, rather than a week consisting of 5 half-days. This would, e.g. true of certain types of shift workers (though "split shift working" would seem better suited to half days), and where "journey to work" times are relatively long.

Proposal 2. *"Resource Kitty Bargaining"*
*An Expenditure Programme for the Public Services*

The context in which this proposal is put forward needs to be emphasised:

a. Heavy unemployment – approaching 1½ million seasonally adjusted – involves heavy additions to public expenditure costs. In considering the total Exchequer cost of high unemployment it should also be recognised that there is a severe loss of tax revenue from earned income that would have been secured had higher levels of employment been secured.

b. Consequently, additional public expenditure of a fairly labour-intensive kind involves relatively low *net* costs to the exchequer.

c. But in addition, the cost of such provision to the wider national economy is exceptionally low under present conditions of under-employment of resources, since in the main the additional resources, required would have continued unemployed or under-employed. Moreover, balance of payments costs are likely to be limited, and the trend of the payments balance does not make this a major constraint.

d. The general position, so far as public expenditure is concerned, is well known: cuts in public expenditure programmes drawn up earlier, and widespread use of cash limits.

e. In the view of TURU there is also the likelihood of under-spending in some public services (notably local government) because of major falls in the cost of debt servicing, due to the steep decline in short term interest rates in 1977 – as compared with those prevailing in 1976-77 and likely to have been assumed for budget purposes for 1977-78. The importance of this can be seen when it is recognised that local authority temporary debt is over £4 billion and loans for less than one year are an important element in their so-called longer term debt.

f. Thus it is unlikely that the proposal outlined below would lead to a breach of the IMF agreement limits on the public sector borrowing requirements fro 1977-78, even if there is any merit in maintaining the IMF loan arrangement.

*The Proposal*

i. The Government should allocate as a first tranche of additional resources (say) 1 per cent on the current cost of a particular public service, or of central Government grant to Local Authorities, to support additional selective public service expenditure projects. These projects would not necessarily have to be "temporary" in nature.

ii. The Government should specify the requirements they would expect projects to fulfil to attract financial support. The "criteria" that might be employed are discussed in the subsequent section of this paper. For Local Authority projects the level of financial support offered might range between (say) 60 per cent and 100 per cent, depending on discussion on the contribution the authority itself might make to project finance. In current circumstances it would be important to add as rider that Local Authorities would need to demonstrate that they were not unreasonably restricting their budgeted expenditure.

*Procedure*

i. The preferred procedure should be the joint submission of specific project proposals by the public service concerned – normally the regional or relevant local level authority – and the appropriate trade unions. The projects would be submitted to the sponsoring Department. Normal trade union negotiated pay structures and conditions of service would apply.

ii. Projects could also be put forward unilaterally for sponsoring Department consideration by public agencies or by appropriate groups of trade unions. But there should be a requirement that serious consultation should have taken place between trade unions and the agency or authorities concerned, and the comments of the "other side" should be sought.

*Criteria*

The approach suggested seeks to bring to the stimulation of public sector expenditure projects a broadly equivalent style to that involved in the Selective Investment Scheme for manufacturing industry. As with that scheme, for administrative purposes the process might initially concentrate on larger projects (e.g. £1 million p.a. or more, or the creation of 200 jobs or more). It is suggested that the criteria to be used to give authorisation and priority to any particular project should include:

- A clear indication of the *cost effectiveness* of the project including (a) associated improved use of existing resources (of capital and labour), and (b) tangible improvements in the quality or range of services to the public.
- Employment creation especially that providing work for the structurally unemployed (i.e. occupations, age groups, or localities subject to persistently high unemployment; priority to longer term unemployed, etc.).
- Minimal call on any scarce resources and low import content.
- Early start.
- Other efficiency savings or financial contribution (including absorption of some or all of the administrative cost of projects) to reduce the net cost in relation to the benefits derived.

**Proposal 3.** *Extending Shift-working in Manufacturing**

Currently, in mid 1977, there are half a million fewer workers in employment in manufacturing than there were before the 1975-76 recession. A

*This proposal was first included in an article in *Personnel Management*, May 1977.

third of a million of the registered unemployed are workers from manufacturing industries. Unemployment is heavily concentrated on manual workers, so that it would be particularly beneficial to develop proposals that could create more manual jobs in manufacturing.

It is not enough to rely simply on "more investment" to create manufacturing jobs. In most parts of manufacturing a massive amount of new investment is associated with each job created; directly, or indirectly, accelerating (and selectively aiding) new investment may displace other jobs in manufacturing.

This proposal suggests, instead, that it could be helpful in terms of employment creation to look more closely at the organisation of shift work in the manufacturing sector.

The extent of shiftworking in manufacturing industry is mainly an indicator of capital intensity. The variations are extreme: two-thirds of men manual workers in iron and steel production receive shift premiums, compared with only three per cent in timber and furniture manufacturing. For women workers the food industry emerges as the one making most extensive use of shiftworkers, though important developments in shift systems using part-time workers are not officially monitored.

Why should a deliberate encouragement of the extension of shift working in manufacturing look attractive?

First, increased shift working can offer an early and sizeable increase in employment in relation to the existing capital stock, as demand for UK goods and services (e.g. export demand, import substitution) develops. The potential improvement in utilisation of the capital stock through shift work, as an almost immediate resource gain, contrasts with the lead time associated with meeting demand solely through increased fixed capital investment (and the additional equipment may have a high import content).

Then, depending on demand conditions, significant gains in capital productivity and economies in capital costs per unit of output may result. Thus even if there are additional costs from accelerated recruitment and training, or enhanced shift pay, the overall result could avoid cost inflation.

Another factor to be considered is the wealth of experience already available in manufacturing industry in relation to the transition to new shift working arrangements, the elements of collective bargaining involved and the management of particular shift systems. Besides, the approach could be flexible in terms of creating both full-time job opportunities and part-time ones. (Some industries whose labour requirements are contracting, e.g. steel, textiles, have made widespread use of shift working in the past, so that the workers concerned may have adapted more to the social problems associated with shift working.)

*Permanent Policy*

Indeed rather than creating more continuous shift cycles with all the social problems that entails, it might be sensible to concentrate on the evolution of double day shifts or on part-time labour. Both of these avenues would be helpful to women, and they represent a potentially permanent type of employment policy rather than a temporary device.

Lastly, insofar as government aid and encouragement is concerned, the approach could be selective, and both the criteria to be used and the kind of aid offered could be influenced by sector working parties and other elements of the government's 'industrial strategy'.

This approach, then, could be linked to selective government aid in helping step up desirable product development and associated marketing effort, and in financial support for increased working capital needs, especially where increased shift work would aid the balance of payments. Indeed, the recently announced Selective Investment Scheme would appear to be directly applicable to the support of employment creation through increased use of shift work. The TUC recently suggested that the government should offer an employment subsidy on net creation of jobs in manufacturing industry; given the improvement in public finances (increased revenue, reduced social security expenditure) from increased employment, there is obvious merit in such proposals.

What sectors might be involved? How important could this be? Sector working parties in wool textiles, knitting, non-ferrous foundries, rubber processing, and printing machinery, among others have all mentioned the need for more shift work. Information on shift premiums available in the New Earnings Survey makes it clear that shift working has only been deployed to a limited extent in many other important export (or import substitute) industries, e.g. many sectors of engineering. As to scale, even an increase of no more than 10 per cent in the number working on shifts would raise employment by over 100,000.

Collective bargaining, now it is free from restrictive limits, can play an important part. Pay policy is now flexible enough to encourage serious bargaining over the terms on which trade unions in particular circumstances may co-operate in the extension of shift work, or accept a variation in previous shift-work systems. New Earning Survey studies indicate that widespread overtime is a feature of much of the shift-work of many industries; perhaps trade union negotiators should give more priority to the limitation of such persistent overtime working by shift workers, and put more emphasis on reduced hours and increased holiday provision as part of the "premia" that shift workers secure in compensation for the "unsocial" aspects of shift work.

The various institutions of the industrial strategy (not least the tripartite machinery of NEDO) ought to be looking at the problems and prospects of employment creation through shift work in the manufacturing sector.

# 15 An Alternative Economic Strategy

**Stuart Holland**

Stuart Holland teaches economics at the University of Sussex

The IMF loan, for which so much was 'sold' was less than the total handout through tax relief on stock appreciation – i.e. a new Labour measure – which has amounted already to £3.8 billions.

The case against the public expenditure cuts should be related to the changed structure of big business since the war: i.e. that 100 companies command some half of manufacturing output and employment, and more than half our export trade, against only some fifth to a quarter of output and employment 30 years ago.

This new monopolistic structure has meant that they now can pass on either cost increases (commodities, oil) from abroad, or pass on the higher unit costs of under-utilised plant, fixed interest borrowing via banks and bonds (rather than variable cost borrowing via the stock market) etc. Big business is now in a position to raise prices to compensate for lost sales, and tends to do with an ineffectual prices policy administered by a government which has no real information on the costs and profit structure of firms. In short, the greater the deflation (through public expenditure cuts) the greater the inflationary pricing by the big business commanding half our activity (to compensate for lost cash flow from sales).

Thus, firms could bring down their unit costs (i.e. production costs per unit of output) if there is more output: i.e. by reflation. Therefore, the key short to medium term policy should be a restoration of the projected reduction of public expenditure (i.e. 'reverse the cuts') plus price controls. Firms who are 'pinched' or squeezed initially will be squeezed less the greater the recovery of demand and output. Those big firms facing bankruptcy or closures if they cannot raise prices by more than an established norm should be able to come and 'reveal' their cash needs to the government via Planning Agreements in which the books concerned are also opened to the unions. Smaller firms (less than £50 millions turnover a year) could be given higher price norms for an initial period (i.e. 18 months).

This would give a rationale for two specific demands:

1. Reverse the cuts in public expenditure.
2. Enforce progressive price controls.

It clearly could be related to a further demand.

3. No further redundancies for the coming 18 months (i.e. for the period in which restoration of demand via public expenditure, and recovery of higher viability through easier covering of fixed costs by business). The rationale here has been admitted by the Temporary Employment Subsidy, which could be allowed to all non-Category 1 firms, with the others going through tri-partite Planning Agreements.

Otherwise, one could also argue the case in both Labour's Programme 1976 and the TUC Economic Review for £1 billion a year expenditure – rather than funds in the kitty which are not used – by the NEB. i.e.

4. £1 billion a year expenditure by the NEB (average year to year) to 1980.

The NEB remit could be linked to taking over those firms which are clearly in difficulties and need diversification and modernisation. Plus a further demand (again in Labour's Programme and the TUC Economic Review 1977), i.e.

5. Planning Agreements negotiation to be started from now, with both an opening of the books to unions and a Social Audit published on the top 100 companies (as promised in Labour's Programme 1973). Plus
6. Establishment of a National Planning Commission and a Cabinet Committee for Economic Planning – which it would serve – as in Labour's Programme 1976.
7. Co-ordination of the Planning Agreements information and projected expenditure by the top 100 plus companies in the Planning Agreements system by the National Planning Commission, using existing potential sanctions such as the Price Code (tightened where

necessary below the allowed national norm for recalcitrants), and the discretionary powers allowed to the Secretary of State for Industry under both the 1972 and the 1975 Industry Acts.

8. A publication of the sectoral and regional distribution of both public expenditure and big league private company expenditure as a term of reference for new debate and claims on resources by both unions and local authorities.
9. Labour Party NEC sponsorship of a national debate on the distribution of employment, between firms and industries, and between regions, i.e. national debate on the case for a 35 hour week, related to the new national planning objectives and institutions.
10. The re-introduction of effective taxation on the big league corporate sector, which, through tax relief on stock appreciation, depreciation allowances, etc., is at present not paying effective tax (i.e. nominal tax is rebated via tax relief).

Such effective taxation will become more feasible with the reflation of public expenditure and demand, covered by the improvement of the trade balance via oil.

We might add the principle of no public money rebated to the private sector from the initial negotiation of Planning Agreements, unless need is revealed via Planning Agreements, as specified as Party policy in Labour's Programme 1973.

The principle might be jargonised as 'no tax relief without representation', i.e. representation of revealed need.

The 35 hour week could, and should, be stressed to relate to the trend to technological unemployment, rather than a cutting of work and pay. This, of course, depends on reflation rather than deflation.

In addition, we could propose a variant on generalised import controls, i.e.

11. The planning of trade via Planning Agreements with the top 100 companies which account for more than half our export trade, plus temporary and selective import controls in some sectors of the economy, with the selectivity focused against classic dumpers or major net export countries, such as Japan. Plus
12. The call on EEC member states to reverse their present 'beggar my neighbour' policies of self-cancelling export surpluses, with a claim that the Federal Republic of Germany in particular should reflate.

In sum:

1. Reverse the public expenditure cuts both to reflate demand and defend the welfare state;

2. Enforce progressive price controls;
3. No further big business redundancies for 18 months, with NEB intervention where necessary;
4. £1 billion a year NEB spending to 1980;
5. Obligatory Planning Agreements negotiations between company unions and governments with top 100 firms;
6. Establish a National Planning Commission, linked to Cabinet, NEDCs, etc., as Planning Agreement co-ordinator;
7. Publish national planning targets, negotiated by unions;
8. Negotiate industry and regional targets with company unions and local authorities;
9. Promote national debate on 35 hour week, related to the 'right to work' and the 'right to income'.
10. No big business tax relief without Planning Agreements negotiation;
11. Plan foreign trade via Planning Agreements with big business and selective, temporary import controls versus developed country imports;*
12. Call on joint reflation via restoration of public expenditure from the EEC Nine.

*I am not wholly persuaded about the import controls case, which is always isolated by the press, but it may be necessary.

# 16 What, Then, Must We do Next?

**Ken Coates**

Clearly, the remedies propounded in this last section of our book all suffer from particular weaknesses. Either they are designed for application by a special group, and therefore of restricted efficacy, or they are capable of wider implementation only when more intractable problems of political agency have been solved. If a sustained campaign were to be mounted for the 35-hour week, if overtime were to come under attack, of course the results could be spectacular: but we must be aware of the considerable difficulty which exists, even outside a time of economic stringency, in giving teeth to such demands.

Moving from limited demands to overall ones appears simple only if we are prepared to ignore the major problem, which is that the Labour Movement, the only imaginable vector of reform on the needed scale, has already been entrapped by a series of Labour Government decisions which have effectively traded in the post-war consensus upon which rested Butskellism, the commitment to welfare, and so many of the key assumptions which have moulded British politics for the past three decades. Any realistic programme of regeneration of employment therefore manifestly depends upon a capacity to recapture Labour's political arm for commitments which, yesterday, were unquestionable axioms, and today have become, for all officialdom, unutterable heresies.

We shall not succeed in this difficult effort unless we combine two arms of a pincer movement. One of these arms involves a passionate agitation for do-it-yourself remedies like the 35-hour week, without which it will be impossible to generate mass political pressure. The other requires alternative national policies, many of which are easily comprehended, but difficult to enforce within a polity containing numerous powerfully undemocratic elite strongholds.

For the first of these purposes, the Full Employment Seminar evolved a short list of immediately practicable agitational calls, which were published as a "Charter of Demands":

> "To counter the deliberate creation of unemployment and to stop its disastrous effects upon human welfare and social advance, the Full Employment Campaign calls upon your organisation – Trade Union, Community Group or other voluntary association – to take one or more of the following actions:
>
> 1. join with others in your workplace and locality to defend employment opportunities against redundancies, especially of those most at risk in areas, industries, occupations and communities afflicted by high unemployment;
> 2. join with others in your region to research and prepare alternative plans for creating new employment opportunities in private and public services, especially for the growing number of young people and women seeking work;
> 3. require full advance information disclosure of future employment plans – one year to five year – by all employing organisations in your area, with full publicity of likely trends;
> 4. demand as a condition for all government aid and tax concessions the signing of planning agreements, involving national unions, joint union committees in in companies, the government and the large companies, to control company investment and trade policies;
> 5. demand increased use of government funds, government controls and government purchasing power to maintain employment on producing goods and providing services that people need at home and for sale abroad;
> 6. establish international links with trade unions and other organisations overseas, especially in the Third World, which are attempting to defend and advance workers' rights against super-exploitation;
> 7. resist public expenditure cuts and demand the development of public service employment to meet the growing need for housing, education, health and environmental improvement;
> 8. reduce the working day and working life of full-time workers, and oppose any return to casual employment."[1]

In this spirit, at the time when this Charter was presented to delegates to the 1977 TUC, we emphasised both types of response:

> "The TUC meets at a time of severe crisis for the Labour movement. Unemployment passed the level of 1,600,000 in July 1977, thus confirming the serious warnings which had been given by all the responsible economic forecasters.
>
> The resolutions which affiliated unions have put forward to Congress reflect a very proper concern about this grave problem.
>
> Two overwhelming considerations should be borne in mind by delegates when voting on this crucial question:

1. We should place a premium on do-it-yourself remedies because they can be set in train immediately. For this reason, demands for the 35 hour week are of vital importance, as are all those other demands which involve the creation of job opportunities.
2. Although we must all continue to press for economic expansion and for greatly increased investment, we must combat the notion that these will automatically solve the problem. They won't. There is a lot of evidence which shows that serious investment programmes tend to reduce the numbers of job opportunities, and to produce redundancies and lay-offs. In the long-run, if there were a dramatically booming economy new job opportunities might be created. But in a context of general international uncertainty it is absolutely clear that this will not happen by itself.

The only short term guarantee of job creation which is practical is the guarantee of new jobs in necessary public service work.

It becomes daily more important that the trade union movement should make a united demand for the expansion of public expenditure, at the same time that it presses for adequate investment programmes under public control. In the present day, cuts in social services and welfare expenditure are the height of folly and cruelty."[2]

For the second arm of the pincer, a convergence of ideas and political mobilisation will be imperative. In addition to developing programmatic demands like those set forth in Stuart Holland's paper, however, it seems vitally important to trigger off the widest possible discussion on the problem, with a view to raising the issue of full employment from the hastily-prepared and unmarked grave which has been dug for it by Authority.

Heaven knows, the evidence of skulduggery is not too difficult to find. Every day, some new official or semi-official statement "sets right" yesterday's assumptions by the simple process of reversing the positive and negative indicators.

On December 2nd 1977, for instance, *The Guardian* reported Sir Ronald McIntosh, the departing director-general of the NEDC, as saying, amongst other things, that "the industrial strategy, even if it is successful, will not lead to any significant increase in employment." But in August 1976 the Department of Employment had issued a handsome broadsheet (Employment News) to inform us that this same industrial strategy, announced in a white paper (Cmnd.6315) the previous November, had, during July and August taken "a key step towards developing Britain into a high output, high wage, full employment economy". NEDC, we were told in this broadsheet, had "decided . . . that in order to improve industrial performance and increase capacity it would be necessary for priority to be given to industrial development." For this reason, after setting up and hearing reports from no less than 37 tripartite sector working parties, industry by industry, "The Government, TUC and CBI made a formal commitment at the August (1976) NEDC meeting to work for the expansion of Britain's manufacturing industry in the period up to 1979." All this was summed up in a neat red-printed panel in the same official handout, telling us that the industrial strategy was "A foundation for full employment."

Clearly, impending retirement wonderfully concentrates the mind. What Sir Ronald told the Institute of Production Engineers at the beginning of December a year later might have been especially commissioned for this book:

> "A high proportion of investment in today's depressed conditions leads to a net fall in employment and, since many firms are hoarding labour, there may be no significant increase in manufacturing employment even when output recovers."

None of this is new, of course: contributors to this volume have been insisting on a similar message for a long time already. But what *is* new is the director-general's solution:

> "Britain should concentrate more on activities which involve higher skills and more value added, ruthlessly abandoning products which fail to meet these criteria."

Sir Ronald's analysis concludes with an emphasis on "the role which service industries will have to play if unemployment is to be reduced to acceptable levels". "Brave words," adds *The Guardian's* reporter to this story "for a man who has been at the centre of the Government's industrial strategy, which is to reverse the decline of manufacturing industry".

However, *The Guardian* man is perhaps a bit over-sanguine about the industrial strategy, which since the intervention of the IMF in December 1976, has been driven fast forward on the pedal marked "reverse". Thus, according to the National Institute of Economic and Social Research:

> "There seems to be in many quarters a belief that the improvement in Britain's economic prospects in 1977 has been almost entirely attributable to our following the IMF 'prescription' of December 1976. We find this contention difficult to accept. The resulting recovery in international confidence, it is true, probably arrested the decline in the exchange rate. But the improvement in the visible balance of payments between 1976 and the first ten months of 1977 (for which we now have official statistics) was largely attributable to oil, and the progressive reduction in the rate of inflation has been largely due to the success of Stage 2 of the pay policy and to the stabilisation and subsequent decline in world (and hence UK import) prices. The major effect of the observance of the Letter of Intent – and in particular of the PSBR limits – has been to ensure an increasingly restrictive fiscal stance which has depressed output, inhibited

industrial investment, and further increased unemployment. Indeed, the one IMF prescription which we wholeheartedly supported – the commitment to manage the exchange rate so as to preserve competitiveness – is the one which has been explicitly abandoned."[3]

The social implications of all these baleful trends are rather dreadfully simple and clear. Some of the main relevant questions are posed in Frank Field's most useful recent study *The Conscript Army,*[4] which prepares a searing indictment of the effects of mass unemployment, not from emotional interviews, but from a veritable blizzard of carefully sifted cold facts. A whole batch of comfortable myths are frozen stone dead as a result.

The recent costs of unemployment are truly staggering: while the dole queues have trebled in length since 1974, nationally we have borne losses of £1,300 million to the Inland Revenue, £940 million to National Insurance, £1,100 million disbursed in flat-rate unemployment benefit, £219 million in earnings-related payments, a billion in supplementary benefit, vast withdrawals from the redundancy payments fund and more than a quarter of a billion's worth of administrative costs. To all this can be added whatever might be guessed as the value of the lost output which has been forfeited by million-fold enforced idleness.

Probing behind these national statistics, Clare Denneling and Jill Sullivan, in a contribution to the same work, take a close look at poverty and unemployment in Liverpool. The unemployed there, they found, shared with those still in work some appalling conditions. But whilst those in jobs could afford remedies, however partial, the unemployed suffered all the ill-effects of damp, cold, and dilapidation. In 20 economically-argued pages, they furnish an absolutely damning refutation of the specious arguments of those who justify unemployment as a legitimate weapon in the fight against inflation.

All this is a clear argument for a full social audit, in which the total weight of unemployment can be assessed by public opinion. If the General Council were to read this most cogent section of Field's book, and join to it the evidence marshalled in these pages, surely they would feel compelled to agree to invite the Labour Party to join them in undertaking a full public enquiry into this whole problem.

By now trade union involvement in agencies like the Manpower Services Commission, or the National Economic Development Council could enable a whole series of probing questions to be posed. A co-ordinated drive to do this might both improve the information flow to a social audit, and at the same time turn each of these official bodies into a platform from which the case for full employment could, with varying degrees of public coverage and response, be most strenuously argued.

"Why bother?", some people will say. We need to bother, because the economic Establishment have up to now succeeded in covering up all the main truths about the sea-change which the return of mass unemployment will imply for all our lives. While the press lords tell us that the whole problem is laziness, or child-centred schools turning out unemployable children because the cane has been locked away, even more sinister voices can be heard blaming the blacks, and bidding up the demand for scapegoats.

At the present time, nobody in authority will make any pledge at all about when 1974 levels of employment can be restored. The Treasury and their dupes have, in fact, successfully shattered the post-war accords which rested all British politics on the platform of full employment. Only a most strenuous campaign, mobilising both the evidence and the people, can restore the basis of civilised living in this battered, injured country.

A full social audit, dramatising the evidence and its meaning, might begin the struggle to form a public opinion capable of such an immense effort.

FOOTNOTES

1. *Labour Leader,* September 1977.
2. Full Employment: Bulletin of the IWC, 1977.
3. *National Institute Economic Review,* November 1977, p.4.
4. Routledge and Kegan Paul, 1977.

# Further Reading


Beveridge, W.H. (1944) *Full Employment in a Free Society,* London, Allen & Unwin.

Boulet, J. and Bell, A. (1973), *Unemployment and Inflation,* London, Economic Research Council.

Bosanquet, N. and Doeringer, P.B. (1973), 'Is there a dual labour market in Great Britain?' *Economic Journal,* June.

Bowers, J.K. and Harkness, D. (1974), 'Duration of unemployment by age', *School of Economics Discussion Paper Series,* 8, University of Leeds.

Bowers, J.K. and Harkness, D. (1976), 'A time series of duration of unemployment by age and sex', *School of Economics Discussion Paper 27,* University of Leeds.

Brittan, S. (1975), *Second Thoughts on Full Employment,* London, Centre for Policy Studies.

Cheshire, P.C. (1973), *Regional Unemployment Differences in Great Britain,* Cambridge, CUP.

Community Development Project Reports, *Guilding the Ghetto* (1977), London, Home Office, *The Costs of Technical Change* (1977), London, Home Office, *Workers on the Scrapheap* (1977), Birmingham, Home Office, *Youth on the Dole* (1977), Birmingham, Home Office.

Community Relations Commission (1974), *Unemployment and Homelessness,* London, HMSO.

Cox, S. and Golden, R. (1977) *Down The Road,* London, Writers & Readers Co-op.

Cripps, T.F. and Tarling, R.J. (1974), 'An analysis of the duration of male unemployment 1932-1973', *Economic Journal,* June.

Daniel, W.W. (1974), *A National Survey of the Unemployed,* London, PEP.

Department of Employment Gazette.

Field, F. (1977), *Are Low Wages Inevitable?* Nottingham, Spokesman.

Field, F. (1977), *The Conscript Army,* London, Routledge & Kegan Paul.

Gordon, D.M. (1972), *Theories of Poverty and Underemployment,* Lexington, Mass., Lexington Books.

Hill, M.G., Harrison, R.M., Sargent, A.V. and Talbot, V. (1973), *Men Out of Work,* Cambridge, CUP.

Holland, Stuart (1975) *The Socialist Challenge,* London, Quartet.

Holland, Stuart (1975) *Strategy for Socialism,* Nottingham, Spokesman.

Keynes, J.M. (1936), *The General Theory of Employment, Interest and Money,* London, Macmillan.

Labour Research.

Lebergott, S. (1964), *Men Without Work,* New Jersey, Prentice-Hall.

Marsden, D. and Duff, E. (1975), *Workless,* Harmondsworth, Penguin.

Meacher, M. (1974), *Scrounging on the Welfare,* London, Arrow.

Mukherjee, S. (1974), *There's Work to be Done: Unemployment and Manpower Policies,* Manpower Services Commission, London, HMSO.

Mukherjee, S. (1976), *Unemployment Costs,* London, PEP.

Murray, R. *The Anatomy of Bankruptcy,* Nottingham, Spokesman.

Pigou, A.C. (1933), *Theory of unemployment,* London, Cass.

Smith, D.J. (1976) *Some Facts of Racial Disadvantage,* London, PEP.

Townsend, P. (1970), *The Concept of Poverty*, London, Heinemann.

Trade Union Research Unit, *Prices, the Next Stage,* (March 1977); *The 1977 Budget: The Real Picture; Economic Strategy and the Sterling Crisis* (Economic Appraisal No.17), *Unemployment – What Next?* (Economic Appraisal No.20), *Can We Live with Single Figure Inflation?,* (Economic Appraisal No.21). Ruskin College, Oxford.

Wedderburn, D. (1965), *Redundancy and the Railwaymen,* Cambridge, CUP.

Wedderburn, D. (1964) *White collar Redundancy*, Cambridge, CUP.

Worswick, G.D.N. (ed.), (1976), *The Concept and Measurement of Involuntary Unemployment,* London, Allen & Unwin.

Wootton, B. (1974), *Incomes Policy, an Inquest and a Proposal,* London, Davis-Poynter.